Contents

Introduction

Well here it is at last, my cookery book. It was a bit of a race against time to get it finished. I was determined that I would give you the real thing and so I have spent many, happy hours checking the recipes. I've taken all the photographs myself, to simply give you a clear and uncluttered view of what the recipes will look like. This was my first attempt behind the camera and I think you will be able to plot my way through the book as my skills progressed!

I kept thinking of more ideas I wanted to add, but the book ended up with too many pages. I had to start collecting for the next book, the eternal optimist that I am! I do hope you enjoy the dishes that you create with the help of this book and that you are inspired to have fun, to experiment and even to write your own recipes!
It has been a wonderful learning curve writing my book, I can't wait to start the next one! There are so many people who have coaxed, cajoled and bullied me through!

Thanks go to:
Sarah (Editor!) and Tom (IT Director!) for having faith in their Mum to do this, for cracking the whip and keeping me here at the laptop, for finding things when I lost them off the screen, for talking me through the simplest of computer operations many times without getting totally frustrated with me, and for giving me lots of hugs, love and understanding throughout the last year. Thank goodness their English is better than mine, as they proof read the chapters! Adding several thousand full stops as they went!

Dear Barbara, who kept the home clean and tidy despite the heaps and piles of papers and general disarray everywhere, for not turning a hair at the expletives as they issued from the office and for being constant source of moral support and so often a sounding board and tasting panel! Also for letting her teddy bears picnic with me beautifully! (In the photographs!)

Anna for typing recipes over the years to build up the lists - otherwise it would have been years before you saw this book!

And finally my late Mum, who passed down lots of her delicious recipes to me and who let me create chaos in her kitchen and who insisted that I went to college to learn to cook properly and train to be a demonstrator. That gave me the opportunity to meet all you wonderful people who have been to my demonstrations and actually wanted these recipes out of my head and told me to write this book for you. So here it is - you'd better buy it now! If you are reading this you probably have, so THANK YOU, have fun and ENJOY!

The list of other people who've helped is very long, so I've just listed all your names here:

Alison, Auntie Edie, Bev, Carol and Bunny, Charlie, Chuff, Claire, David , Diane, Erin, Heather, Janine, Jen, John, Katy, Kaye, Keith, Lawrence, Lee, Marilyn, Mary, Meg, Nicky, Nina, Pam, Richard, Sally, Sam, Steve, Stuart, Sue and Tim.

Also all the wonderful staff at all the venues I work at, your support has been amazing and I can never thank you all enough.

January

January always seems a bit of an anti-climax after Hogmanay welcomes in the New Year. I've decided to cheat by putting Hogmanay recipes here, as they seem to get overlooked by all the Christmas festivities and everyone's New Year resolution to go on a diet after all that over indulgence!
(But it was delicious at the time!) Hogmanay recipes are well worth breaking that resolution for and cheering up a dreary January.
I like to do a Hogmanay replay for Burns Night, 24th.January. It's a good excuse to have a party and make everyone wear tartan, even if it is only a pair of socks and a hanky! If you have a Scottish friend, it will be their duty to address the Haggis (address included but not the dirk for the stabbing!). Mock Haggis is very easy to make, but the authentic Scottish made Haggis is readily available from your friendly local butcher if you ask him nicely! All you then have to do is simmer it gently for the allotted time, which leaves you free to try an interesting selection of superb malt whiskeys to compliment the feast! The recipes use ingredients that are prime Scottish produce.

RECIPES

Smoked Salmon Towers

Leek and Stilton Soup

Curried Haddock Flan

Mock Haggis

Kidney's Flambé

Cabbage Pie

Cranachan and Flummery

Shortbread

Linzer Torte

Whiskey and marmalade bread and butter pudding

Jane's Fruity flapjack

Pam's Marmalade

Scottish Smoked Salmon Towers

Smoked Salmon is a staple standby for an instant light meal.

You could smoke your own - there are home smokers available and it adds a new dimension to the supermarket salmon! It's even better if you can catch your own salmon, they can usually arrange to smoke it for you when it is freshly caught in this case though.If you are lucky enough to have a local fishmonger, cultivate his friendship to guide you to best buys and when is a good time to stock up and do a little smoking. He can also save your time by filleting the fish for you when necessary!

This is a great recipe as you can use off cuts and trimmings that are often available for dishes such as this, mousse, soufflé and pâté. It combines salmon with orange and walnuts (home grown ones have dried by now) to add a little crunch with some sweetness from the brioche toast.

Ingredients:

300g. Smoked salmon trimmings
30g. Chopped walnuts
1dsp. Walnut oil
Zest and juice of an orange
1tsp. Chopped chives
1tsp. Chopped dill OR parsley
Seasoning
6 slices Brioche
6 tsp. Crème fraîche
6 Quail eggs
3tsp. Caviar (OR golden salmon eggs OR lump fish roe)
Chives and dill or parsley to garnish
A few rocket leaves
A dressing made with walnut oil and balsamic vinegar, seasoning and a few chopped walnuts.

Method:

1. Trim and chop the salmon. Place in a bowl with the chopped walnuts, orange rind and zest. Add the herbs of your choice, seasoning and the walnut oil. Mix well together and allow to chill in the refrigerator for an hour at least before shaping.

2. Divide the mixture into 6 even portions and press each portion into a 5cm pastry cutter and push out onto a plate cover and chill again until needed.

3. Cut the brioche into 5cm circles and toast it. Place a portion of salmon on each circle. Top this with a teaspoonful of crème fraîche with half a quail egg and a little caviar at the side of the egg. Sprinkle over some chopped herbs.

4. Place the tower in the centre of the plate with a few salad leaves around it and trickle over the dressing.

5. You can serve with extra toasted brioche.

Leek & Stilton Soup

This is an alternative to the salmon and the usual Cock a Leekie soup laced with prunes, that is normally served at Burn's Night. It is time to use that Stilton left over from Christmas! It is always at it's best at this time of year and, as I am always tempted to buy too much, this is a delicious way to use it up!

Ingredients:

600g Leeks
1 Large potato
30g Butter OR 2tbs. Oil
300ml Stock
300ml Cream- single or double
1 rounded tsp Cornflour
100-200g Stilton cheese
Black pepper and ground nutmeg to season
Chopped parsley to garnish

Method:

1. Trim and wash the leeks thoroughly. Slice the leeks finely and peel and slice the potato.

2. Heat the butter or oil and sauté the leeks and potato gently until they start to soften. Add the stock and simmer until the vegetables are cooked.
Do this in the simmering oven of the Aga.

3. Slake the cornflour with a little of the cream and then add the rest of the cream and stir this into the soup and heat through.

4. Crumble the Stilton into the soup and stir as it melts, taste and add pepper and nutmeg if necessary to YOUR taste. As cheese tends to be salty, it is not usually necessary to add any salt.

5. Sprinkle over the chopped parsley just before serving with lots of warm bread.

Curried Haddock Flan

This is one of those reliable recipes that you come back to again and again. I love the flavour of the little smokies, but you can use the larger smoked haddock if you have trouble finding the Smokies.

You could also try smoked salmon steaks, which are now available. To cook the steaks, cover them with milk or water with a bay leaf, a few peppercorns and some parsley stalks. Bring the liquid to the boil, then take off the heat and put to one side and leave to cool. The fish will cook in the liquid.

I serve this as a starter, a light lunch or as supper dish with just a good mixed salad.

Make the cheese pastry according to the recipe opposite and line a 24cm flan dish or tin with it.

Ingredients:

1 Onion - chopped
1tbs. Butter
1tsp. Curry Powder
1tbs. Double Cream
1tbs. Milk
2tbs. Mango Chutney
2 Eggs
3or 4 Arbroth Smokies - cooked, skinned and broken up
Parsley to garnish
Another 100ml.Cream.

Method:

1. Peel and finely chop the onion.

2. Melt the butter and sauté the onion gently. Add the curry powder and cook for 2 minutes. Then add the cream and milk and simmer slowly until well reduced.

3. If the chutney has large chunks in it, chop it up more finely. Add this and the haddock to the cream mix.

4. Beat the eggs with the 100ml of cream and pour over the filling in the pastry case and cook.

5. **Aga:** On the floor of the roasting oven for approx. 20-30 minutes until well-risen and golden brown.

   Electric: Fan oven 170°c (Gas mark 6) for 30-40 minutes. Heat a baking tray first and cook the tart on this to help cook the base of the tart.

   If you have an oven with just bottom heat cook on 200°c for 40-45 minutes until the pastry starts to shrink from the sides of the dish or tin.

Cheese Pastry

Ingredients:

250g. Plain flour
100g. Cold butter
100g. Grated strong flavoured
cheese e.g. Cheddar
1/4tsp. Cayenne pepper
1/2tsp. Mustard powder
1/4tsp. Salt
1Egg yolk made up to 50ml with
water or all water – about 2 tbs.

Method:

I use the food processor to make
the pastry

1. First grate the cheese finely
   in the processor, remove the
   grater disc and the cheese
   and put the central blade
   in the bowl.

2. Cut the cold butter up into small
   pieces and add it to the flour,
   cayenne pepper, mustard and
   salt in the bowl. Process it until it
   forms fine breadcrumbs, add the
   grated cheese and then pulse to
   mix through.

3. Mix together the yolk and water
   and add to the processed
   mixture with the motor running,
   As soon as it starts to bind
   together stop the motor, remove
   from the bowl and knead gently
   to a smooth paste. Cover with
   cling film or put in a polythene
   bag and chill in the refrigerator for
   30 minutes before rolling it out to
   line the flan dish or tin. See rolling
   tips later in this chapter.

This makes a rich, short pastry,
which can also be used for cheese
biscuits or as a base for canapé.

Mock Haggis

Firstly apologies to my Scottish friends, but this is a very simple recipe for a Mock Haggis. The ingredients of Haggis are a well guarded secret, it is probably better that we don't know, but this is a rather tasty alternative. Serve with the neeps and tatties.
The barley and oatmeal are available from some supermarkets, or health food shops.

Neeps and Tatties
The traditional accompaniment to haggis is well mashed potatoes and well seasoned neeps. There is a great debate as to what neeps are. I think it is a regional problem - neeps I think is short for turnip. I call the small white fleshed root turnip and the orange fleshed root a swede and it is the swede that is cooked and mashed with lots of butter and black pepper. I also add a half tsp sugar to the swede with the salt as it cooks. If you mix the two mashed vegetables together, it is then called Clapshot, and don't ask me why! Just enjoy they are an excellent foil for the haggis.

Ingredients:

50g. Pearl or pot Barley
100ml. Stock
200g. Lambs or pigs liver
200g. Pork sausage meat
200g. Best minced beef
175g. Chopped onion
2tbs. Chopped parsley
1/2 tbs. Chopped sage
30g. Pinhead oatmeal or this is also called medium cut oatmeal
30g. Butter, lard or oil
A dash of Worcestershire sauce
1/2 tsp. Cayenne pepper
Salt and freshly ground black pepper
A 15cm x 25 cm approximately boil in the bag-bag

Method:

1. Pour the boiling stock over the barley and leave it to soak for at least an hour.

2. Sauté the onion with the butter, until soft.

3. In the food processor mix the liver, sausage meat and mince. Remove to a bowl and add all the other ingredients. Mix well by hand, it's just easier but not essential to the recipe, you can use a wooden spoon! Season well with plenty of black pepper and salt.

ADDRESS TO A HAGGIS

Fair fa your honest, sonsie face,
Great chieftain o' the pudding-race!
Aboon them a' ye tak your place,
Painch, tripe, or thairm:
Weel are ye wordy o' a grace
As lang's my arm.

ROBERT BURNS

4. This amount fills a 15cm by 25cm bag. This is an easy way to cook the haggis. Put the mixture in the bag and tie up the opening. Fill a saucepan with 4-5cm of boiling water and a small trivet in the base so that the bag is not sitting on the bottom of the pan. Lower the bag into the saucepan and cover the pan with a well fitting lid. Bring it back to the boil and simmer for about 2 hours.

Aga: Cook in the simmering oven once it has come back to the boil. Alternatively you can bake the haggis in a loaf tin.
The disadvantage is that this doesn't look like a Haggis, but it still tastes good! Lightly cover it with butter paper or foil. Cook in the roasting oven for 20 mins and then a further 45-60 mins in the simmering oven, until it is firm to the touch.

Electric: Simmer gently simmer on the hob or cook in an electric fan oven 160°c(Gas mark 4) for 1-1¹/2 hrs.If cooking in a tin. You can let the haggis cool in the bag and then reheat simmering for 30 mins, or you can serve it straight away with neeps and tatties.

15

Kidneys Flambé

A delicious, quick savoury at the end of a meal or snack, if you like kidneys. At this point I must make a confession, there is very little offal that I do like, but I will cook it for others and I am assured it really is delicious. It certainly smells good!

If you want to devil the kidneys, add 1tbs whole grain mustard (seedy, I usually call it at demonstrations!) and a good dash of Worcestershire sauce as you add the cream. "Devilled" the kidneys make a great wake-me-up breakfast. They can also be served in a scooped out bread roll.

Ingredients:

4-6 Kidneys (2 Lambs kidneys per person as a savoury)
Enough milk to cover the kidneys
2 Spring onions
1 Clove of garlic (optional)
20g. Butter
1tbs Oil
1/2 Lemon
Cayenne pepper
Salt
1tbs Chopped parsley
3 tbs. Brandy
2tbs. Double cream
Fried bread or toast

Method:

1. Cut the kidneys in half, remove the core and the outer skin and cover with the milk (the milk helps to extract any impurities.) Leave the kidneys to soak for about 30 minutes. Make the fried bread , cut into neat triangles and keep it warm.

2. Chop up the spring onions and the garlic. Melt the butter with the oil in a small frying pan and fry the onions and the garlic for 2 minutes so they start to soften.

3. Lift the kidneys from the milk and pat them dry on kitchen paper. Cut each kidney into about 3 pieces and add to the frying pan and cook until brown on the outside but still pink in the middle.

4. Sprinkle the lemon liberally with cayenne and then squeeze over the kidneys. Pour the brandy over the kidney, allow it to heat up and set it alight.
To keep it alight shake the pan gently.

5. As soon as the flames are out stir in the cream and the parsley. Adjust the seasoning to taste if necessary. Serve with the fried bread cut into triangles or make fresh toast.

Cabbage Pie

It just doesn't taste like cabbage! My excuse is that my little hands are too warm for all that pastry folding, so, yes, I buy the puff pastry, sorry!

Ingredients:

1 Small firm white cabbage
70g Butter or 3tbs Oil
150g Mature Cheddar, grated
1 Large cooking apple, grated
Seasoning - Salt, pepper and ground nutmeg go well with cabbage
Egg and milk (egg wash) to glaze
1 Packet ready-made puff pastry

Method:

1. Roll out half of the pastry and line the base of a shallow 25cm pie plate. Roll out the other half for the top.

2. Finely shred the cabbage, discarding the outer leaves and stalk. Melt the fat or oil in a large pan or wok and cook the cabbage for a few minutes until it is just changing colour.

3. Fill the lined plate with layers of the cabbage, grated cheese and the grated apple, seasoning the cabbage well.

4. Brush the outer edges with egg wash and top with the pastry. Seal the edges and make a small hole in the centre. Decorate with the pastry trimmings and brush with egg wash.

5. Cook until a lovely golden brown. Serve with a good chutney or a salsa of red pepper, onion and tomato with a dash of Worcestershire sauce, oil, seasoning, a little sugar and chopped mint!

To Cook

Aga: on the floor of the roasting
oven for 20 -25 minutes

Electric fan oven 180°c (Gas mark
7) for 25-30 minutes
Combination oven 200°c with 360
watt microwave for 20minutes

Cranachan or Flummery

One is made cold with sugar and ginger. The other is made warm with honey and lemon. Both are equally delicious and are very simple to make, but are perhaps not very good for the cholesterol levels!

Cranachan Ingredients:

50g. Pinhead oatmeal, toasted.
3tbs. Whiskey
50g. Stem ginger
25g. Muscavado sugar- light
Pinch of salt
300ml. Double cream

Method:

1. Put the oatmeal in an shallow ovenproof dish and toast in the oven shaking occasionally, OR grill under a hot grill stirring to brown it evenly OR shake over high heat in a frying pan until the oatmeal is a rich golden brown. Tip it out onto a piece of kitchen paper to go cold.

2. Chop the stem ginger into smallish pieces

3. Whip the cream until it is just holding its shape.

4. Fold all the ingredients into the cream.

5. Spoon into pretty glasses to serve with shortbread.

6. If you have any crystallized ginger, put a piece on the top with a small basil leaf!

Flummery Ingredients:

300ml. Double cream
3tbs. Clear honey
Zest of 1/2 a lemon
3tbs whiskey or whiskey honey
liqueur
1tbs Toasted oatmeal

Flummery with Cox's

An alternative is to serve the
flummery with dessert apples

Ingredients:

3 Apples
Butter
Honey OR Muscavado sugar
Lemon juice

Method:

1. Liberally butter 6 ramekin dishes

2. Peel and core the apples and
   slice in half into two rings. Place
   an apple ring in each dish, add a
   large teaspoon of sugar or honey
   over the apple.
   Then squeeze over a little lemon
   juice.

Bake

Aga: On the floor of the roasting
for 10 minutes
Electric fan oven 180°c (gas mark
7) for 10-15 minutes

Method:

1. Whip the cream until it just holds
   its shape.

2. Gently heat the honey in a
   saucepan, or warm on the back
   of the Aga, or in a microwave for
   30 seconds on 600 watt. Fold it
   into the cream and add the
   whiskey and the lemon zest. It
   may go runny, don't worry! Serve
   in small glasses or dishes with
   the toasted oatmeal sprinkled
   over the top. Serve with
   shortbread.

3. Remove from the oven as the
   sugar is starting to caramelize.
   Allow to cool then turn out onto a
   plate or they can be served in
   the ramekins with the flummery
   on top.

3. Spoon the flummery around the
   apple and sprinkle with the
   toasted oatmeal. Decorate with
   a couple of basil leaves, if they
   are available, as the taste goes
   rather well. Serve with the
   shortbread.

Shortbread

My Mother made the best shortest shortbread. She was English to the
core, but I suppose the recipe was originally Scottish! My sister still
makes this recipe weekly and there is always some in the tin - this is one of
the joys of going to visit!
She gets top marks every time she enters the local show, so it is always
slipped into the group theme each year! When Mum first made it she used to
use butter made from whey, which is a by-product of cheese making.
I'm not sure that this is available, so just good British butter works well.

Ingredients:

200g. Butter
100g. Caster sugar
200g. Plain flour
100g. Rice flour, or you can use
ground rice or semolina which will
give a grittier texture,

Method:

1. Cream the butter and the sugar
   together until they are pale, light
   and fluffy.

2. Sieve together the flours into the
   bowl and fold into the creamed
   mixture. Knead lightly to a
   smooth ball and allow to rest in a
   cool place for at least 30
   minutes.

3. Roll out onto a well floured board
   and cut into fingers or rounds.
   Line a baking sheet and place
   the shortbreads on this to cook.
   Alternatively you can line a flan tin
   with bake-o-glide and press
   about 1cm depth of mixture
   evenly into the tin. Turn this out
   on to the baking tray and cut into
   approximately 8 slices -
   petticoat tails!
   Prick well with a fork and cook

4. **Aga:** In the baking oven on the
   grid shelf on the floor of the oven
   for about 20 minutes
   Or on the grid shelf on the floor
   of the roasting oven with the cold
   shelf on the second shelf from
   the top for 15-20 minutes until
   still pale with just a soft tinge of
   colour coming through.

   Electric fan oven160ºC
   (Gas mark 4) for 20-30 minutes

5. Remove from the oven, allow to
   cool slightly and cut into slices
   while still warm. Dredge lightly
   with caster sugar. Put onto a
   cooling rack once firm to cool
   completely. Store in an airtight
   container.

Linzer Torte

A Classic! A non-cream pud, a rather smart jam tart, and what little boy can resist a jam tart! It uses a very rich nut pastry. Which nuts you use is up to you. I use walnuts when I have a glut of walnuts, but whichever nuts you use, use them with their skins on as this gives the traditional look to the tart - it's a good source or fibre too! The filling can be fruit packed home made, or quality bought jam. Alternatively you can use 450g of fresh or thawed frozen raspberries whizzed in the food processor with 100g Mucavado sugar, I like to then sieve it, but it isn't compulsory!

Ingredients:

120g Plain flour
120g Castor sugar
120g Butter
120g Ground hazelnut
Flavourings - A pinch each of ground cinnamon and ground cloves and salt
2 Egg yolks
50g Jar of raspberry jam OR
450g Raspberries and 100g Sugar made into puree

Method:

1. Place the whole nuts with their skins on in the processor bowl and whiz until thoroughly ground, but not so long that they go oily.

2. Add the flour, sugar, flavourings and the butter (cut up into small pieces). Process until you have fine breadcrumbs and then with the motor still running add the egg yolks. Switch off as soon as it starts to bind together.

3. Remove from the bowl onto a floured board. It will be very soft, so gently draw it together into a dough. Cover it and chill for a good hour. If you leave it for longer let it come back to room temperature after you remove from the refrigerator so that it doesn't just break up as you roll. It is better too soft than hard to handle.

4. Roll out three quarters of the pastry to line the 20-24cm flan tin or dish. Chill for a while as you roll out the remaining pastry into a strip as long as the width of your flan tin. Cut the strip into smaller strips 1-2cms wide.

5. Half fill the pastry with jam or raspberry puree and lattice the top with the pastry strips.

6. Brush a little egg yolk over the strips of pastry.
There should be enough yolk left in the container that the yolks you used in the pastry were in for this.

7. **Aga:** Cook on the floor of the roasting oven for 15-20 minutes if it is in a tin. A ceramic dish may take longer
(20-30 minutes).

   Electric fan oven, on a preheated baking tray 160°c (Gas mark5) for 45 minutes - 1 hour.

8. Remove from the oven. Allow to cool. Remove the outer ring if in a flan tin. Dust with icing sugar before serving,
Serve just warm as jam can burn straight from the oven.
Accompany with yogurt, cream or custard is good!

Rolling tips for lining flan dishes or tins

1. Roll the pastry out gently on a well-floured board turning the pastry a quarter turn after each roll until it is the right size. Roll it up carefully round the rolling pin and unroll it into the tin, easy! See picture 1A & B

2. Flan Tin
   If you have a loose bottomed flan tin, remove the base and roll the pastry over the base, trim round and place this back in the ring. Roll the remaining pastry into a sausage the length of the perimeter of the tin. Lay this in the tin around the inside edge. Press with the fingers up to the top edges, joining the bottom edges as you go. See picture 2A.

3. Take the required amount of pastry, flatten it into an easy to handle round and place in the centre of the tin and gently work it to the sides and then up to the top edge, keeping the thickness as even as possible, no rolling pin necessary! See picture 3A.

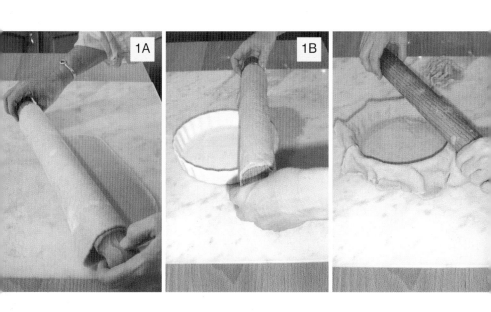

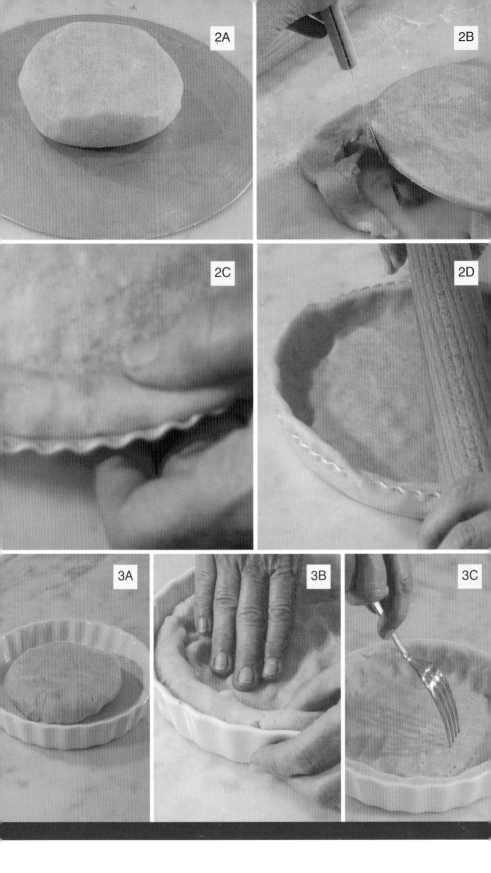

Whiskey & Marmalade Bread & Butter Pudding

An eternal favourite with lots of variations which you'll find throughout the book. This one has whiskey, as a concession to Hogmanay, but add your own favourite tipple or none at all or orange juice - cook it as you like it, that is what cooking is all about!

Ingredients:

8-12 Rounds of bread and butter
Marmalade
300ml. Cream
2 Large eggs
4tbs. Whiskey
50g. Sultanas
30g. Demerara sugar

Aga: Cook on the grid shelf on the floor of the roasting oven for 15-20 minutes.

Electric fan oven 170°c
for 20-25 minutes
Combination oven 200°c
and 180 watt for 12 minutes.

Method:

1. Soak the sultanas in the whiskey for at least an hour if possible.

2. Butter a shallow ovenproof dish.

3. Spread the marmalade onto the bread and butter. Arrange a single layer of bread in the dish and sprinkle over the sultanas and then put another layer of bread in the dish.

4. Beat together the cream and the eggs and pour it over the bread. The pudding is always better if it is left it to stand for 30 minutes before cooking.

5. Sprinkle over the demerara sugar, this give a crunch to the top, and cook.

Jane's Fruity Flatjack

I think all of you who have seen me demonstrate must have tasted this flapjack. It is the easiest and most popular tray bake. My family only like gooey flapjack, but just cook it longer if you want it crisp. No two flapjacks are the same; it includes whatever is in the store cupboard and is just as good if it is made with just oats!

Ingredients:

350g Butter or margarine
225g Demerara sugar
2 tbs Golden syrup, honey or maple syrup.
370g Rolled porridge oats
100g Jumbo oats
200g A selection of Pumpkin seeds, sunflower seeds, linseed, mixed fruit, chopped nuts or dates or dried mango, papaya or crystallized ginger
OR you can just add 675g of rolled porridge oats to make a plain flapjack.

To Cook:

Aga for 15-30 minutes on the grid shelf on the floor of the roasting oven. Put the cold shelf on the second set of runners to stop it getting too brown after about 15 minutes OR on the bottom set of runners in the baking oven for 20 -40 minutes

Electric fan oven160°C for 30-40 minutes

Method:

1. Melt together the butter or margarine with the sugar and the syrup or honey in a large bowl, in the microwave for 3 minutes at 800watt OR in the simmering oven of the Aga OR on the hob in a large saucepan. Then stir in the dry ingredients thoroughly.

2. Line a large roasting tin with bake-o-glide and tip in the flapjack mix. Level out with a wooden spoon and press it firmly down.
   Bake until it is cooked how you would like it, gooey or crisp - just cook it longer for crispy.

3. Remove from the oven and allow to cool slightly and then with a blunt knife (so as not to cut the bake-o-glide) cut into fingers. Allow to become cold and break into pieces and store in an airtight container.

Pam's Family Marmalade

I make small amounts of marmalade now and then. We have never been great marmalade people, but Pam, a life long friend who went to college with me and helps with my demonstrations at home, makes kilos of the stuff. She has to, because it is so good it always disappears very quickly! She has kindly agreed to share it with you. So here it is as she gave it to me.

SEVILLE ORANGE MARMALADE
This is a recipe that has been used by both my mother and grandmother very successfully for many years. It is kept in the back of a very battered and loved edition of the Aga cookery book that came with my Aga 30 years ago.

Ingredients:

9 Seville oranges
2 Sweet oranges
1 Lemon
$3^{1}/2$ kgs. Warm granulated sugar
4 litres Water

Method:

1. Peel the oranges and finely shred the peel (I have an ancient marmalade cutter for shredding the peel. The peel and pith can be put through the mincer or that attachment of a food processor or mixer very successfully, this makes a more chunky marmalade.)

2. Remove the pith. Shred half of the pith and add to the peel, put the other half in a separate bowl.

3. Cut the oranges in half and remove the pips and membrane to the separate bowl containing the pith and add 500ml water.

4. Place the peel, fruit and juice in the preserving pan. Add $3^{1}/2$ litres water and leave to soak overnight.

5. Tie up the pips and pith etc. in a muslin and add these to the preserving pan. Bring to the boil and boil for an hour (this could be done in the simmering oven of an Aga)

6. Remove the muslin and its contents. Squeeze out the juice as this contains a lot of pectin (setting agent).

7. Warm the sugar this helps it to dissolve more quickly. Add the warmed sugar to the mixture and return it to the boil. Boil for 40 minutes.

8. Test the mixture for setting point by placing a small amount on a saucer. When it is cool draw your finger through the surface. If a skin has formed the marmalade can be potted, allow it to cool slightly. Stir it well just before potting to stop the fruit from rising to the surface.

9. This makes 14-16 jars of marmalade.
   This amount needs a large preserving pan - mine is 12 pint and is not really big enough - Mother's is 24pint and is brilliant!

Thank you Pam!

February

A romantic month with Valentines Day and expensive red roses! More often than not it includes Pancake Day and the start of Lent, so let's eat all the things we shouldn't before we give them up for Lent!

RECIPES

Pancakes in all shapes and sizes

Basic batter

Assorted Stuffed Pancakes savoury and sweet

Pancake Meringue Cake

Wild rice pancakes

Breakfast Bacon pancakes

Cheesy fruity pancakes

Red pepper Soup

Herby scones

Love Apple Tartlets

Pork chops

Omelette Confiture

Hearty Banoffi Bread and Butter Pudding

Angle Cake Surprise

Chocolate caramel bars

Pancakes

I never seem to eat many pancakes on Shrove Tuesday - I'm too busy making them for everyone else as they sit waiting forks poised! There is something rather good about plain, really thin pancakes served with caster sugar or golden syrup and a generous squeeze of lemon juice, but the basic pancake is a good starting point for both savoury or sweet fillings and toppings. I have listed some of my favourites below.

Pancake batter Ingredients:

100g Plain flour
1Egg
300ml. Milk
Knob of butter
Pinch of salt

Method:

1. I always do pancake mix in the food processor. Put all the ingredients in the bowl and whiz. Leave to stand in the processor for 30 minutes, then pulse for a second and pour into a jug.

2. Lightly oil a hot pancake pan or frying pan. Pour in about 2 tbs of batter, swirl it around to cover the pan with a thin layer. Cook on one side and toss and cook the other side. Keep warm on a plate covered with a cloth or an up turned plate.

Filling suggestions:

Savoury

A rich white sauce with smoked fish, prawns, dressed crab, lobster or salmon, herbs and cheese or left over meats.

A thick tasty mince.

Left over meats with savoury marmalade.

Cream cheese and blanched vegetables, with a little curry powder.

Spread the filling in the pancake and roll up, serve individually, or line up in a baking dish, pour over a little more sauce or grated cheese and just brown in the oven or under the grill.

Sweet

Jam, syrup, or chocolate spread or fresh fruits with stem ginger and a little sugar, with cream cheese, cream or ice cream.Just roll it up in the pancake!

Or

Fold 4 pancakes in the hot pan with a knob of butter, add liqueur or spirit of your choice and flambé, serve with clotted cream or ice cream.

Pancake Meringue Cake

Ingredients:

8 Pancakes x 20 cm
A Jar of lemon curd (or jam or soft fruits)
100g Ground almonds
2 Egg whites
100g Castor sugar

Method:

1. Put a cooked pancake on an oven-proof plate and spread with a thin layer of lemon curd. An optional extra is to sprinkle over some ground almonds. Repeat until you have a neat pile of pancakes, finishing with a pancake.

2. Make the meringue: Beat the egg whites until really stiff. Divide the sugar into three lots, add the first lot to the egg and beat again. Add the second lot, beat really well again and finally fold in the remaining sugar and any ground almonds that are left over.

3. Spread the meringue all over the pancakes and brown in a hot oven and serve immediately.

To cook

Aga: cook in the baking oven on the grid shelf on the bottom set of runners for 15 minutes

Electric fan oven170°c(Gas mark 6) for 10-15 minutes

Wild Rice Pancakes

I first made these little pancakes in Canada. Canada is one of the world's largest exporters of wild rice, which isn't a rice at all but the seed of a water grass, originally harvested by the native Indians from their canoes.
They make an interesting appetizer, as the pancake has more texture than the usual scotch pancake recipe.

Ingredients:

100g Cooked wild rice
30g Whole-wheat flour
40g Self raising flour
1/2tsp Salt
1/2tsp Sugar
1/2tsp Baking powder
1/2tsp Bi-carbonate of soda
100ml. Buttermilk
1 Egg
1 Spring onion finely chopped
1 tbs Chopped parsley or coriander
To Finish:
Crême fraîche or cream cheese
Smoked salmon, caviar, boiled quails eggs, prawns, crispy bacon or vegetables

Method:

1. Separate the egg. Sieve together the dry ingredients, add the yolk and the buttermilk and mix well together.

2. Add the cooked rice, spring onion and herbs.

3. Beat the egg white and fold into the mixture.

4. Cook spoonfuls of the batter on a hot iron griddle plate or directly on the simmering plate of the Aga, turning each one as the bubbles burst.

5. Allow to cool wrapped loosely in a tea towel.

6. Serve with some crème fraîche or cream cheese, topped with a twist of smoked salmon or whatever you choose!

Breakfast Bacon Pancakes

Ingredients:

4 Rashers streaky bacon
1 Egg
4 tbs Milk
2 Spring onions chopped
1 tbs Chopped parsley
Self Raising Flour
1 tsp Baking powder
Salt and pepper
100g Mushrooms

Method:

1. Cut up the bacon up into small pieces and lightly fry.

2. Beat the egg and add the milk, chopped onion, parsley and seasoning.

3. Sift in the flour and the baking powder add the fried bacon and stir together.

4. Slice the mushrooms and cook in the bacon fat, left in the pan from cooking the bacon.

5. Drop spoonfuls of the batter onto a griddle pan or the Aga simmering plate, cook on both sides until golden brown.

6. Serve topped with mushrooms (you could cook tomatoes instead of mushrooms) or a fried or poached egg or just buttered, as breakfast in one hand! Eat straight away.

Cottage Cheese Pancakes

These give a sharp contrast to fresh fruit, but can also have a savoury filling, the pancakes have a very soft texture.

Ingredients:

1 Egg
200g Cottage Cheese
65g Self Raising Flour
40g Butter

Fruit for filling
Segments of orange or mango or any soft fruit
Cream cheese or crème fraîche
Icing sugar to dredge over the pancake

Method:

1. Put all the ingredients for the pancakes in the bowl of the processor and whiz until well mixed. Allow to stand for about an hour, pulse and remove from the processor and cook spoonfuls on a griddle plate (a frying pan will do) or directly onto the simmering plate of the Aga.

2. Put a layer of cream cheese on the pancake and top with some fruit, fold over the pancake or if you have made small ones, leave the pancake flat and top with another pancake and dredge heavily with icing sugar. Serve warm.
Can be served cold, in which case only top just before serving.

Red Pepper and Tomato Soup

This has been my favourite soup as long as I can remember. It freezes well and if you are on a fat free diet, just miss out the butter and the sautè stage. Soups are so easy and such good value, using vegetables, straight from the garden with herbs and seasoning. Simmer slowly and extract all the flavour, leave it as a wholesome chunky soup or liquidize for a smooth soup. If it's a tomato soup, I normally sieve it after liquidizing to remove the seeds.

Ingredients:

1 tbs Butter
1 Onion
2 Red peppers
1x 450g Tin tomatoes or 6 fresh tomatoes
1 litre Stock
2 tbs Tomato puree
A handful of fresh parsley and one of basil
2 Sprigs of thyme
2 Bay leaves
1 tsp Sugar
Salt and pepper
To serve a little single cream

Method:

1. Melt the butter in a good sized saucepan. Chop the onion and the peppers. Sauté and once they are soft add the other ingredients. Bring to the boil, reduce the heat and simmer slowly for about 45 minutes - this can be done in the simmering oven of the Aga.

2. Allow to cool. Remove the bay leaves and the thyme sprigs, liquidize and sieve to remove the seeds. Reheat and serve with a swirl of cream - in the outline of a heart for Valentine's Day - your red heart! Scatter some torn basil leaves on top. The cream isn't essential but it's pretty! Herb scones go well with this soup.

Herb Scones

Ingredients:

225gms Plain flour
1 tsp Bicarbonate of soda
2 tsp Cream of tartar
1/2 tsp Salt
1/4 tsp Cayenne pepper
1tbs Chopped fresh herbs
40g Butter
150 ml. Milk

To Cook:

Aga: Bake in the roasting oven for about 15 minutes for the large round or 8- 12 minutes for the smaller scones.

Electric fan oven 180°c (Gas mark 7) 15-20 minutes for the large round or 10 - 12 minutes for the smaller ones.

Method:

1. Sieve together the dry ingredients into a bowl. Rub in the butter to form fine breadcrumbs.

2. Add the herbs and the milk. Mix these in with a round bladed knife, until it starts to bind together,

3. Remove from the bowl to a floured board and knead lightly together. Pat into a neat round about 1^1/2cm thick and cut into 8 wedges. Place on a floured baking tray and dust with flour ready to cook. You can roll the mix out and cut out small scones with a heart shaped cutter for Valentines Day!

4. Brush the top with milk to glaze, and cook.

Love Apple Tartlets and Variations

These can be neat nibbles or a stunning starter. Tomatoes were called love apples many moons ago, so here they are in February! They are very easy to prepare and the combinations are endless.

Ingredients:

A packet of ready made Puff pastry - can be the ready rolled variety!
Pesto or tomato puree
Cherry tomatoes
Fresh basil leaves
Salt and pepper
Olive oil
A little vodka
1 Egg beaten with 2 tbs. milk to glaze

Method:

1. Roll out the pastry (if not ready rolled). Cut into approximately 8 cm squares or circles - there is more wastage if you cut circles though. A packet of ready rolled pastry that I buy makes 15 neat little squares with no wastage!

2. Press the pastry into bun tins and brush with the egg wash glaze. Put 1/4 tsp of pesto, tapenade or tomato puree in the centre of each square or circle.
Wash and dry the tomatoes and cut a slit in the non-stalk end of the tomato. Slide a basil leaf into it and place it in the centre of the pastry on top of the pesto
Season with salt and pepper and cook.

Aga: Cook on the floor of the roasting oven for 8-10 minutes

Electric fan oven 180°c for 15 minutes

3. Allow to cool slightly. If you have a syringe or dropper fill it with vodka and inject each tomato with a little vodka! This is optional but fun. The tarts can be served hot or cold. For a starter you could serve with a pink tomato hollandaise. (see May)

Variations
to go on the pastry:

Chopped pear and walnuts or pine nuts with crumbled Stilton. You can put pesto or creamed horseradish underneath.

Chopped apple with crumbled Cheshire cheese and some chopped sage, with crab apple jelly underneath.

Sautèed peppers with chilies or anchovy fillets on pesto or tapenade.

Mushroom: remove the stalk from a button mushroom and put a little garlic puree in the hollow. Top with a little oil or butter and lots of black pepper.

3-4 cooked prawns topped with garlic butter with parsley.

These are just a few ideas the combinations are endless! They all work very well on crostini too.

Easy Sweet Pork Chops

Ingredients:

Select the number of pork chops
and for each chop:
1/2 a Dessert apple
2 tbs Soft brown sugar or
Demerara sugar
1 tbs English mustard powder
Optional
1 tbs Grated fresh root ginger-
Zest and juice of a lemon or orange
Crab Apple jelly with ginger
(see September)

Method:

1. If you prefer, remove the rind off
   the chops. Arrange them in a
   roasting tin.
2. Mix together the sugar, mustard
   powder, lemon zest and the
   ginger. Sprinkle over the chop.
   Squeeze over the lemon juice.
3. Bake the chops in the oven for
   30 - 40 minutes depending on
   the thickness of the chops.

Aga: Cook on 3rd set of runners
from the top in the roasting oven

Electric fan oven170ºc
(Gas mark 6)

4. Prepare the apples: cut them in
   half from stalk to eye and scoop
   out the core. This is very easy
   with a melon baller! Put a
   teaspoonful of crab apple jelly in
   the centre of each apple. After
   the chops have had 15 minutes
   cooking time add the apples to
   the tin.

5. Serve the chops with the apple half sitting on top - instant apple sauce! If you want a gravy, the meat juices give a caramely sweet and sour flavour. Serve with simple vegetables, such as creamy smooth mashed potatoes, carrots and cabbage. If you don't want to make gravy, cook some cabbage for just 2 minutes in a good covering of salted water. Drain, but save the water. Make a white sauce with it.

To make the white sauce:

40g Butter
30g Flour
Ground nutmeg and pepper

1. Melt the butter in a saucepan. Add the flour and stir well.

2. Add the cabbage water a little at a time until it coats the back of the wooden spoon.

3. Add $1/4$tsp grated nutmeg and some black pepper. Add the cabbage and stir together, check seasoning and serve.

Omellette Confiture

This recipe is inspired by many happy holidays spent in Alpbach, Austria.
It is a pud to share and they made a wonderful one of these at the Jak
Gasthof there - I hope they still do!

Kaiserschmarrn
Another omelette inspired pudding from Austria is Kaiserschmarrn. For
this,use the same ingredients but do not separate the eggs, just beat all the
ingredients together, then throw in a handful of raisins and cook in the pan.
This is be stirred whilst cooking. When it is just starting to set, pop it in the
oven to firm up for 3 minutes. Then remove from the pan, cut up.
Serve heaped up on the plate.and dredge well with icing sugar.

Ingredients:

4 Eggs
2tbs Self Raising Flour
4tbs Milk (or Cream)
1 tbs Castor Sugar
Butter for cooking
Icing sugar to dredge over
Fruity jam, stewed fruit or puree

Method:

1. Separate the eggs. Beat together
   the yolks with the flour, sugar and
   milk.

2. Whisk the egg whites until stiff,
   but not dry. Fold the two
   mixtures together.

3. Melt the butter in a 30cm frying
   pan. Pour the egg mixture into
   the pan and cook over gentle
   heat for about 3 minutes. Put the
   whole pan in the oven to finish
   cooking, or under a low heat grill
   until lightly brown.

4. Warm the jam or fruit.

5. Slide the omelette out of the pan
   onto a warm plate. Slit the centre
   and pour the warmed jam into
   this. Fold in the two sides and
   dredge liberally with icing sugar.
   Serve immediately.O.K.it is good
   with ice cream as well!

Banoffi Bread and Butter Pud

Two favourites rolled into one. For Valentine's Day the top layer of bread and butter can be cut with a pastry cutter into heart shapes!

Ingredients:

8 Rounds of thin bread and butter
3 Bananas
200ml Fudge sauce
300ml Single cream
3 Eggs
Flaked almonds

To Cook

Aga: Cook on the grid shelf on the floor of the roasting oven for about 20 minutes

Electric fan oven 170°c (Gas mark 6) for 20 -30 minutes
Combination oven 180°c with 180 watt microwave

Method:

1. Butter an ovenproof dish and line with a single layer of bread and butter.

2. Pour over $1/2$ of the fudge sauce.

3. Peel and slice two of the bananas. Arrange over the base layer of bread, then put another layer of bread and butter in the dish. Slice over the third banana and pour over the rest of the fudge sauce.

4. Beat the eggs into the cream and pour over the bread and butter. Allow to stand for at least 30 minutes before cooking.

5. Sprinkle over a generous layer of flaked almonds and bake.

Angel Cake Surprise

I have a heart shaped mould and cook this cake in it for Valentines Day.
There is a swirl of fruit puree through the cake - raspberries out of the freezer,
defrosted and just processed and sieved to remove the seeds, or fresh
strawberries. I don't think there's a month when they are not available from
somewhere! You can actually buy bottles of pureed fruits, which you could
use instead. This makes a light dessert or a good cake for friends for tea!

Ingredients:

60g Plain flour
150g Caster sugar
4 large egg whites
Pinch of salt
1/2 tsp Cream of tartar
1/4 tsp Vanilla essence or Almond
essence
200g Red soft fruit pureed

Method:

1. Sift the flour together with 50g of
   the sugar.

2. Beat the egg whites until foamy.
   Add the cream of tartar and beat
   until the egg whites are stiff but
   not dry. Gradually beat in the
   sugar. Add the flavouring
   essence.

3. Sift the flour onto the mixture and
   fold carefully together.
   Put in a base lined 20cm tin.
   Put a third of the mixture in and
   pour a very thin layer of the puree
   over. Add another layer of cake
   mix and another layer of puree
   and then the final layer of cake
   mix and bake The fruit ripples
   through.

Aga : Cook in the baking oven on the bottom set of runners, for 40-50 minutes , or in the roasting oven for 30-40 minutes on the grid shelf on the floor of the oven, putting the cold shelf on the 2nd. Set of runners half way through the cooking time.

Electric fan oven 160°c
(Gas mark 5) for 30-40 minutes

4. Leave to cool upside down on a cooling rack until cold and loosen the edges and remove from the tin, serve dusted with icing sugar.

Chocolate Caramel Bars

These used to be a regular in the cake tin, but I stopped making them for the same reason that I left the chocolate tasting club - they are too moreish and too fattening! They are a very enjoyable indulgence though.

Ingredients:

For the shortbread base:

125g Margarine or butter
60g Caster sugar
150g Plain flour
50g Rice flour
Pinch of salt

Caramel:

110g Margarine or butter
110g Castor sugar
170g ($^{1}/_{2}$ a 397g.tin approximately) condensed milk
2 tbs Golden syrup

Topping:

200g Chocolate - melted

Method:

1. To make the shortbread base: cream the butter and sugar together until light and fluffy. Mix in the flours and salt - it will bind together to a firm paste.

2. Line a small shallow baking tray (30cm x 20cm) with bake-o-glide. Press the shortbread into the base of the tin and bake.

Aga: Cook on the grid shelf on the floor of the roasting oven for 10 - 15minutes.

Electric: Fan ovenat 170°c (Gas mark 6) for 15-20 minutes

3. Allow to cool, while you make the caramel, the easiest way to make this is in the microwave
Put all the ingredients for the caramel in a large bowl and microwave at 800 watt for 3 minutes and stir well, then microwave at 600 watt for 5 minutes. Stir at least once during this period.

4. If you don't have a microwave, put the caramel ingredients in a saucepan and melt stirring all the time. Bring to the boil and boil for 5 minutes, stirring frequently.

5. Pour the caramel over the shortbread base and spread out evenly. Allow to go cold before pouring over the melted chocolate. Give the tray a shake to smooth down the chocolate. Let the chocolate set before cutting it into bars or squares. Store in an airtight tin, out of sight - otherwise you will eat them all!

March

Easter and thoughts of Spring around the corner , a Good Friday picnic, to find a mountain or beach or river and have a picnic with a game of football or rounders to keep everyone warm! Chickens, fish, rabbits and Easter Eggs.

RECIPES

Dipperty Do's

Savoury Souffles Cooked Once or Twice

Fish Turbans

A Really Good Fish Pie

Sausagemeat Plait

Gingery, Mustardy, Nutty Rabbit

Chicken Breasts stuffed with Stilton and Herbs

Or With Coconut, Ginger and Lime

Nina's Stuffed Aubergines

Chocolate Peppermint Squares

Simnel Cake

Bakewell Tart

Meringue Chicks

Easter Egg Bread and Butter Pudding

Dips

These really are very easy to make yourself, and their flavour and texture are far superior to the bought ones. First, you need a base such as soft cream cheese, mayonnaise or Greek yogurt (it is thicker than the ordinary kind). To this you can add whatever you fancy out of the refrigerator.

Method:

The method couldn't be simpler - just mix all the ingredients together (I sometimes do this in the food processor). Check seasoning, allow to chill a little and serve with crudités.

A few of my favourites are:

Pink dip:

150g Cream cheese
100g Cooked prawns chopped or smoked salmon or a packet of ready-made smoked salmon pate.
1tbsp. Chopped coriander, dill or parsley
A dash of Tabasco or chilli powder
1/4tsp Cayenne pepper
A squeeze of tomato puree or ketchup
Zest and rind of lemon

Tuna dip:

A tin of tuna -drained, or a packet of tuna pate
Capers and parsley go well with tuna or/and a teaspoon of cumin. For extra bite you can add some chopped jalapeno!

Mushroom dip:

A packet of mushroom pate, add the cream cheese or mayonnaise with 2 cloves of crushed garlic or 3cms. Garlic puree. 1 tbs. Chopped parsley and lots of black pepper.

Mediterranean dip:

With your chosen base add some chopped up antipasti red peppers or sun dried tomatoes out of a jar, with some chopped green or black olives and some chopped spring onions or chives, plus extra herbs if you like. A little pesto or tapenade or chilies or a few chopped anchovies can also be added and lots of garlic of course!

Curry dip:

If you are in a hurry, add curry powder to the base with zest and juice of a lemon or lime, a tbs. of mango chutney (or apricot jam!) and chopped chives. A tbs. of desiccated coconut adds texture too. If you have more time, sauté a chopped onion in a little oil and add the curry powder to cook for a few minutes - this gives a better curry flavour.

Ham dip:

Chopped up ham with a tbs. Cumberland sauce with onion and whole grain mustard added to the cream cheese.

Stilton dip:

Stilton added to mayonnaise with some chopped walnuts and chives. Of course you can use lots of other cheeses, just use your favourite and enjoy!

Beetroot dip:

Use cream cheese as your base, add well-chopped beetroot with a generous dollop of horseradish and a dash of Worcestershire sauce.

Almond and cranberry dip:

100g Toasted flaked almonds
30g Butter
60g Fresh cranberries
100g Cream cheese
Salt and pepper
This is a great one for Christmas. Just sauté the almonds and cranberries in the butter, allow to cool, and mix with the cream cheese and the seasoning. It's delicious with celery as a dipper, or you could chop some up finely and add to the dip to add texture. Orange zest is good in this too.

I could go on and on but I think that you will have got the idea that if you have a base ingredient then you can always create a fabulous dip.
Create your own and let me share your ideas!
Serve with a good assortment of cruditès vegetables, cheesy biscuits
 and crispy things.
All these dips can also be used as toasty topping with extra grated cheese on top and just grilled or browned in the oven, or as sandwich fillings, cold or toasted, or as sauces with fondue.

Hot Savoury Soufflé including Twice cooked soufflé.

To give the soufflé more flavour, the milk can be infused with a small onion, a carrot, a stick of celery, 2 cloves and a blade of mace. Put all these in a saucepan with the milk, bring almost to the boil and put to one side to allow the milk to absorb the flavours, strain and use the tasty milk to make the sauce. This method can be used when making any savoury white sauce. Add vegetables, herbs or spices that complement the dish that you are cooking to the milk before you make up the sauce with it.

The soufflé can be cooked in a 2 litre soufflé dish, if you are only cooking it once, instead of the ramekins.

Ingredients:

30 g Plain flour
40 g Butter
150 ml. Milk
4 Large eggs
100 g mature cheese- grated
1 tsp. Dry mustard powder
Cayenne pepper and salt
Butter for greasing to soufflé dish
About 2 tbs. Fresh bread crumbs
(An added twist frozen ice cubes of Bloody Mary's)

Method:

1. Grease 6 ramekin dishes with the butter and coat with the breadcrumbs. Separate the eggs.

2. Make a panada (a thick white roux sauce with egg yolks added). Melt the butter in the saucepan and add the flour, stirring all the while with a wooden spoon. Then gradually add the milk until you have a thick smooth sauce (if milk is warm it will blend in more easily). Season well with cayenne pepper and salt and allow to cool a little before beating in the egg yolks.

3. Add the cheese and the mustard powder. Check seasoning.

4. Beat the egg whites until stiff but not dry. Add 2tbs. of the beaten egg white to the sauce, fold together and then add this to the rest of the sauce. You will find it will fold in more easily because they are similar textures.

5. Place carefully in the prepared dish, no more than 2/3rds full. And cook.

Aga, on the grid shelf on the floor of the roasting oven for 15-35 mins, or 30-40 mins. for a large soufflé, until well risen and golden brown.

Electric fan oven170°c (Gas mark 5) for 20-30 mins for small ones or 40-50 mins. for a large soufflé.

Serve IMMEDIATELY, with garlic bread and salad.
An interesting twist to the ordinary soufflé is to slip an ice cube of bloody Mary mix into the centre of the soufflé just before you cook it; it melts to give a rather yummy tomato sauce in the soufflé (see above). Alternatively some sautéed onion or mushroom (or both) could be placed in the bottom of the dish before the soufflé mix.

Twice Cooked Soufflé
Extra Ingredients:
300 ml. Double cream
3 cloves of garlic- crushed
About 3tbs. Grated Parmesan and another tablespoonful for topping.

Once the small soufflés are cooked and cooled, run a knife around the edges to loosen the soufflè (if you are really worried about this you can base line the soufflé dishes.)
Turn them out onto an ovenproof serving dish, mix together the cream and garlic and cheese and pour this over the soufflès. Sprinkle over the remaining grated parmesan.
You can add cut-up cooked ham or prawns with some parsley if you want to make a more substantial meal and mix this in with the cream.
Reheat in a hot oven for about 15 mins. until the cream is bubbling, serve with garlic bread and a simple salad.

Fish Turbans

This recipe is suitable for any thin fillets of fish such as whiting. For years my son would only eat whiting and strangely every white fish seemed to change into whiting as I cooked it! Plaice, sole or trout as in the recipe all work really well.

Ingredients:

2 Trout Fillets
4 Large Tomatoes
50g Butter
Chopped Dill or Parsley
Zest of 1 lemon
2 Slices of bread made into breadcrumbs
Salt and pepper
Watercress to serve on - optional

Method:

1. Cream the butter with the lemon zest and herbs of your choice. Add a little seasoning and mix in the breadcrumbs.

2. Skin the fish , follow the pictures on the following page to help skin the fish.

   If they are very wide cut the trout fillets in half lengthways.

3. Spread the butter mixture onto the skin side, roll up towards the tail with the top side on the outside.

4. Remove top from the tomatoes and scoop out the seeds

5. Place the rolled up fish in the tomato shell and bake in a buttered ovenproof dish.

To cook

Aga in the baking oven for 20 mins.
on the third set of runners

Electric fan oven160°c
(Gas mark 5) for 20 mins.

Serve on a bed of watercress
with hot fresh bread.

A Really Good Fish Pie

The pie can be as rich or as simple as you like. It has been one of my favourite recipes for years and is always polished off so it must be quite good! This is the first time I have ever written the recipe down so I hope that I have remembered all the ingredients, not that it matters too much as it is very versatile and can be altered according to one's likes and dislikes. You can change the peas for fresh raw asparagus, sweetcorn, broccoli, lightly sautéed chopped red peppers or mushrooms! Just a little of what you fancy or what happens to be in the refrigerator or store cupboard. The mash can also be added to with some chopped spring onions or sautéed garlic, or top it off alternatively with seasoned fresh breadcrumbs with some grated cheese and herbs added.

Ingredients:

1kg. Assorted fish - anything that you enjoy, for example smoked haddock, cod or smoked salmon steaks with fresh haddock or cod and assorted shelled shellfish.
Milk to cover
Bay leaves, lemon peel. blade of mace, parsley and a few peppercorns and a small onion chopped

For the sauce:

To every 150ml of cooking liquid add:
25g Plain flour
30g Butter
Approximately 100g Cheddar type cheese optional
50g Frozen peas
A hard boiled egg
1 tbs. Chopped parsley
1 Egg
500g Cooked potatoes
Butter

Method:

1. Place the selected uncooked fish in an ovenproof dish. Add the bay leaves, peel, mace parsley, peppercorns and onion, cover with milk and place in the oven;

    Aga on the grid shelf of the roasting oven for about 15-20 mins, depending on the amount of fish.

    Electric fan oven 160ºc (Gas mark 5) for 20 mins. Microwave oven 600 watt for 8-10 mins.

2. Remove from the oven and allow to cool in the milk, or until cool enough to handle, remove the skin and bones from the fish and strain the milk.

3. Make a white sauce with the butter, flour and milk . Add the cheese, if using, and adjust the seasoning to taste. Beat the egg and add this to the sauce with all the fish (try not to break it up too much), frozen peas, or your choice of vegetables, chopped hard-boiled egg and parsley. Put in a greased ovenproof dish and top with the potatoes or a breadcrumb mix.

4. The potatoes can either be roughly chopped and mixed with a little more grated cheese and put on top of the fish mixture. Or mashed with a little milk, salt pepper and butter and spread over the fish. Roughen the surface with a fork or pipe the potato on top and cook:

Aga on the grid shelf on the floor of the roasting oven for 30-45 mins. until golden brown and thoroughly heated through (slightly bubbly!)

Electric fan oven 170°c
(Gas mark 6) for 30-45 mins.

To skin fish

Make an incision at the tail end and holding onto the skin at the tail, with firm strokes of the knife pressing down on the skin, work to the other end flicking the skinned fish back as you go, so that you can see where you are.

Sausagemeat Plait

Another test of time favourite! A great lunch or supper dish but it's also excellent eaten cold so it's a must for the Good Friday picnic. And if the wonderful spring sun fails to pop out to encourage a game of football or cricket to keep everyone warm then it's perfect for eating in the car with your fingers.

Ingredients:

1 Packet puff pastry
400gms. Sausagemeat
2-3 tbs. Grated swede
2tbs. Sweetcorn kernels
1tbs. Tomato ketchup or
Worcestershire sauce
1 Hard boiled egg chopped
1 Small onion finely chopped
4-5 Sage leaves chopped or
parsley or thyme or none
1 Egg and a little milk to glaze the
pastry
Seasoning

Method:

1. Put the sausagemeat in a bowl and add the additional ingredients that you like and mix together well, it is easiest to do this with your hands!

2. Roll the pastry out to an oblong and visually divide the pastry into 3 sections. Spread the sausagemeat filling down the centre section, make diagonal cuts from the edge almost to the filling, 2cm apart down each side. Take alternate strips from each side over the filling to form a plait, tucking the top and bottom ends under neatly. SEE PICTURES.

3. Place on a lined baking tray and brush with egg wash (the egg, milk and salt beaten together) and cook.

Aga on the floor of the roasting oven
for about 30 mins. until crisp and
golden brown.

Electric fan oven 170°c
(Gas mark 6) for 30-40 mins.
Combination oven 200°c
with 360 watt microwave for
approximately 20- 25 mins.

Serve hot with vegetables or cold on
its own or with salad.

Rabbit

My daughter will never forgive me for including a rabbit recipe, but it comes to mind when you think of Easter and it is a good meat to try for a change. Rabbit goes well with mustard and ginger, and nuts give texture to a recipe, so ring the changes simply.

Ingredients:

1 Rabbit jointed
100g Pancetta
1 tbs. Flour with salt, pepper and a tsp. of Mustard powder.
2 Cloves garlic
100 gms. Chopped almonds or pine nuts
2 tsp. Grated fresh root ginger
1tbs Cider vinegar
150ml. Ginger wine or red or white wine or cider or ginger beer
1tbs. Chopped parsley
1tsp. Chopped sage
2 tbs. Crème fraîche

Method:

1. Put the flour in a bag and toss the joints in this to coat.

2. Put the pancetta in a pan and cook to let the fat run. Add the rabbit joints and seal on both sides, then throw in the crushed or chopped garlic and the nuts. Cook for a moment or two and add the ginger, herbs and liquids. Bring to the boil reduce the heat and cook very gently for 30 mins. until the rabbit is tender. This can be cooked in the simmering oven of the Aga.

3. Remove the rabbit from the pan and place on a serving dish. Reduce the liquid if necessary and stir in the crème fraîche, taste the sauce and pour over the cooked rabbit. Top with a little chopped parsley and serve with creamy mashed potato and a mixture of quickly cooked vegetables boiled, or stir fried with a little root ginger.

Stilton Stuffed Chicken Breasts

If I have rabbits for Easter I will have to have chicken too! So a couple of different stuffings, always a good contrast of textures and extra flavour to the meat.

Ingredients:

4 Boneless chicken breasts
Stilton stuffing:
 80-100 gms. Stilton cheese
2 Slices of bread made into breadcrumbs
40 gms. Cottage cheese
2 Spring onions chopped
1 tbs. Chopped parsley
1tsp. Chopped thyme
40gms. Walnut pieces chopped-optional
Salt and black pepper
Butter or oil
Wine or water

Method:

1. Wipe and trim the chicken breasts, (you can make this dish with the skin either on or off the joints). Place the breast between two layers of cling film and beat out to make a larger flat piece of chicken.

2. Mash together all the stuffing ingredients, the walnuts are optional as not everyone can eat nuts.

3. Spread a thin layer of the filling over each flattened chicken breast and roll it up loosely and secure with string or cocktail sticks. Chill for at least 30 minutes before baking.

4. Oil or butter an ovenproof dish or roasting tin and place the chicken in this, (if the skin has been removed put a little oil or butter on each piece of chicken or a rasher of streaky bacon) pour about 50 ml. of wine or water into the base of the dish and bake:

Aga on the second set of runners in the roasting oven for 15-20 mins and until the juices run clear.

Electric fan oven 170°c (Gas mark6) for 20-30 mins depending on the size of the joints and until the juices run clear Combination oven 180°c with 360 watt for 15-20 mins.

5. Remove the chicken from the dish. Add a little more wine or water to the dish and loosen the sediment, then pour into a saucepan. Reheat and reduce if necessary, or thicken with 1 tsp. cornflour slaked with a drop of water and added to the boiling liquid, stirring as it thickens. Pour over the chicken.

Serve on mashed potato with wholegrain mustard added and sugar snap peas.

Lime & Coconut Stuffed Chicken

Ingredients:

4 Chicken breasts
50 gms. Butter
1 Small onion chopped
40 gms. Desiccated coconut
The Zest and juice of 1 or 2 limes
1 tsp. Grated fresh root ginger
1 Round of bread made into
breadcrumbs
1 tbs Cut coriander
Butter or oil
White wine, ginger beer or water
Salt and pepper

Method:

1. Wipe and trim the chicken breasts (you can make this dish with the skin either on or off the joints). Place the breast between two layers of cling film and beat out to make a larger flat piece of chicken.

2. Saute the chopped onion with the 50g butter until softened but not coloured. Add the coconut, ginger, breadcrumbs, coriander, seasoning and the lime zest and juice. (Limes can be very hard to extract the juice from, so try putting them in the microwave for 30 seconds at 600 watt to loosen the juice. It works with lemons and oranges too!)

3. Spread a thin layer of stuffing over each flattened chicken breast and roll it up loosely and secure with string or cocktail sticks. Chill for at least 30 minutes before baking.

4. Oil or butter an ovenproof dish or roasting tin, place the chicken in it (if the skin has been removed put a little oil or butter on each piece of chicken) and pour about 50 ml of wine, ginger beer or water into the base of the dish.

Bake:

Aga on the second set of runners in the roasting oven for 15-20 minutes and the juices run clear.

Electric fan oven 170°c (Gas mark 6) for 20-30 mins. depending on the size of the joints and the juices run clear Combination oven 180°c with 360 watt for 15-20 minutes.

5. Remove the chicken from the dish. Add a little more wine or water to the dish and loosen the sediment, then pour into a saucepan. Reheat and reduce if necessary, or thicken with 1 tsp. cornflour slaked with a drop of water and added to the boiling liquid, stirring as it thickens. Pour over the chicken.

Serve on a bed of rice and with a colourful selection of stir-fried vegetables, or your favourite vegetables.

Nina's Stuffed Aubergines

I am very lucky that I love the work that I do. The really big plus of giving demonstrations all over the world is that I meet so many lovely people who will talk cooking and recipes for ever with me. This is when the seeds of many ideas are sown or shared. This is a recipe very kindly shared with me by Nina who comes to demonstrations that I give in Cambridge. I love to try your favourite recipes and this one is a winner and can be used with other vegetables e.g. corgettes, peppers and onions! I must also thank Nina for chivying me along to get my book written so that you wouldn't have to write down the recipes at the demonstrations. I'm not sure that will happen because I do keep changing all the recipes but they are mainly variations on a theme anyway!

Ingredients:

2 Large aubergines
A little oil
250g Mushrooms, assorted or plain.
2 Cloves of garlic
1 Large onion
350g Grated cheese
1 tbs. Chopped parsley

Method:

1. Wash the aubergine and prick with a fork and rub over with oil. Place in the microwave for 3-4 mins on 600 watt to soften the aubergine, or oil and wrap in foil and put in the roasting oven of the Aga for 20 mins. Allow to cool so that they are cool enough to handle.

2. Cut in half lengthways and scoop out the softened flesh from the middle and chop it up.

3. Peel and chop the onion, garlic, mushrooms and aubergine. Put some oil in a frying pan or small roasting tin and sauté the vegetables.

4. Add the grated cheese (keeping a little back for cooking), parsley and seasoning. There are so many wonderful cheeses out there, which all give their own individual flavours to this dish so try a different one each time!

5. Pile the stuffing back in the aubergine "boats" and sprinkle over a little more cheese.

6. Place in an oiled baking dish or tin, add 2 tbs.water, then bake:

Aga roasting oven for 20-30 mins.

Electric fan oven 170°c
(Gas mark 6) for 30 -45 mins.
Combination oven 170°c
with 600 watt microwave for15 mins.

Serve with hot crispy bread
and a salad.

Thank you very much Nina!

Chocolate Peppermint Squares

My son insisted that this recipe was included, as he has enjoyed it for almost 20 years. I hope that some of you enjoy it too!

Ingredients For the base:

150 gms. Margarine
125 gms. Self Raising Flour
60gms. Soft Brown Sugar
30g. Cocoa Powder
85 gms. Rice Krispies (crushed)
1tsp. Baking Powder

For the filling:

440 gms. Icing Sugar
4tbs Water
A few drops of Peppermint Essence
A little Green Colouring if desired

For the topping:

250g Plain Chocolate

Method for the base:

1. Melt the margarine in a bowl on the back of the Aga or in the microwave 360 watt for 1 1/2 mins.

2. Add the flour, sugar, cocoa powder, crushed rice krispies, baking powder and a pinch of salt if you wish. Mix well together and place in a lined, small shallow baking tray or Swiss roll tin and bake:

   Aga for approx. 10 minutes in the roasting oven on the grid shelf on the floor of the oven or 20-30 mins. in the baking oven on the bottom set of runners.
   Electric fan oven150°c
   (Gas mark 3) for 20 mins.

3. Make up an icing with the Icing Sugar, Water and Peppermint Essence (adding the green colouring if you would like it green), and while the base is still warm pour this over the top.

4. Allow this to cool and then melt
   the chocolate on the back of the
   Aga or in the microwave 360 watt
   for 3 mins. Stir until smooth and
   then pour over the peppermint
   mix, shake the tin to smooth out
   the chocolate and remove any
   bubbles.

5. Allow to go cold. Cut into
   squares and enjoy, store in an
   airtight container.

Simnel Cake

I like to have a Simnel cake at Easter. Its origins are varied. Some say that it started life as a cake that young serving girls were allowed to make to take home to their family, when they went home once a year on Mothering Sunday. My family always had a Simnel cake at Easter, the almond paste balls represent the disciples left after Judas had betrayed Jesus at the Last Supper. Whatever the true origins, I shall keep making it as it is a jolly good cake. I love almond paste, but if you don't and you like just a simple fruit cake then leave out the almond paste layer and cook for about 10mins. less (5 mins less at the 90 watt stage for the combi. Cooking).

Ingredients:

200gms. Butter
200gms. Castor sugar
3 Large eggs
250gms. Plain flour
1 tsp. Baking powder
125gms. Currants
125gms. Sultanas
180gms. Raisins
125gms. Glace cherries
125gms. Cut peel
60gms. Almonds chopped or ground Optional
Rind and juice of an orange
500 gms. Almond paste
100gms. Icing sugar

Method:

1. Put all the dried fruit in a bowl; add the zest and juice of the orange and leave to soak overnight.

2. Line an 22-24 cm. tin.

3. Cream the butter and sugar together, beat the eggs in one at a time and fold in the fruit, nuts, baking powder and flour.

4. Roll out 250g of almond paste to a circle the size of the tin.

5. Put 1/2 of the cake mixture in the tin, place the almond paste on this and the rest of the mixture on top and smooth the surface.

6. Bake **Aga:** in the baking oven for about 1 1/2 - 2hours, check after an hour and cover the top with a piece of cardboard if it is brown enough.

Or in the cake baker for the same length of time.

Electric fan oven 140°c (Gas mark 2) for 1 3/4 - 2hours. Combination oven 150°c with two stages of microwave 180 watt for 10 mins. followed by 20 mins with 90 watt.

7. Leave to cool in the tin. Roll the remaining almond paste into 11 even sized balls (these are supposed to represent the remaining apostles, after Judas Iscariot has left the Last Supper to betray Jesus). Place them evenly around the edges of the cake, cover the centre of the cake with foil and brown quickly under a hot grill, or you can use a flame gun to just colour the paste balls.

8. Make a fairly thick icing with either water or lemon juice with the icing sugar, and pour it into the centre of the cake. Put 1/2 a washed egg shell on the icing to act as a vase for some fresh primroses to decorate. Or crystallize some primroses by brushing the petals lightly with egg white and sprinkling with castor sugar, allow to dry on a cooling rack.
Put a band of pretty coloured paper around the outside of the cake and tie a ribbon around.

Bakewell tart

This is a traditional recipe that is a great standby as a pudding or cake and travels well for picnics too. With good pastry and no baking blind, it is a good one to do quickly beforehand and will keep for a day or two. Or make it up and freeze it, rather than cook it and then defrost it, and cook it when convenient if you want to get ahead with dinner party preparation, and then serve it warm.

Rich Short Pastry Ingredients:

340 gms. Plain flour
200 gms. Butter
1 tbs. Icing sugar or castor sugar
2 Egg yolks
1 tbs. Cold water

The Bakewell Tart Ingredients:

Jam red or apricot for the base of the tart
170gms. Butter
150 gms. Castor sugar
130 gms. Semolina
50 gms. Ground almonds
1 tsp. Almond essence
2 Small eggs
100gms. Icing sugar and a few glace cherries for decoration or some flaked alomonds.

Method for pastry:

1. Put the flour, icing sugar and cut up butter into a food processor and pulse until fine breadcrumbs. Then add the yolks and water and pulse until the pastry is forming a ball, remove from the bowl and knead gently until smooth. Cover and chill for 1/2 an hour before rolling out to line the flan tin or dish. Prick the base and allow the case to rest for 1/2 an hour before putting in the filling.

I always make up this amount of pastry, as it will line 2 x20 cm flan cases. I can use one and freeze the other ready for quick use another day. Do take care if freezing in a ceramic flan dish as it may crack if going from different extremes of temperatures too quickly.

Method for Bakewell Tart:

1. In a saucepan melt the butter and sugar together, remove from the heat and add the semolina, ground almonds, almond essence and eggs and beat really well together to a smooth slightly paler mixture.

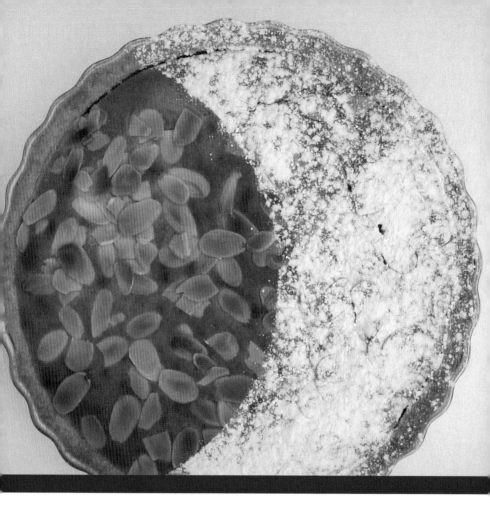

2. Spread the jam on the base of the pastry and pour over the bakewell mixture if baking straight away. Otherwise allow the mixture to go cold before putting it in the pastry case. You can scatter a few flaked almonds over the top for a different finish instead of icing and cherries.

3. Bake straight away:

Aga on the floor of the roasting oven for about 15 mins.and then on the grid shelf on the floor of the oven for another 10 mins put the cold shelf on the second set of runners if it is browning too quickly.

Electric fan oven 170°c (Gas mark 6) for 30-35 mins. Combination oven in a 25cms. Flan dish NOT tin 200°c with 180 watt microwave for 18 mins.

4. Allow to cool. Make up the icing with water and pour over the tart and decorate with cherries or dust with icing sugar.

Meringues Easter Chicks

To use the egg whites left over from making the pastry, make up a meringue mix and make some Easter Chicks.

Ingredients:

2 Egg whites
55 gms. Castor sugar
Yellow food colouring
Red or blue food colouring
Double cream

Method:

1. Put the egg whites in a clean dry bowl and whisk until really stiff. Divide the sugar into 3 portions and add 1 portion and whisk until really stiff, then add the 2nd. Portion and $1/2$tsp. of yellow colouring if you want yellower chicks and whisk again and then fold in the final third. Place in a vegetable piping bag with a 1cm vegetable pipe.

2. Pipe a 5cm round and pull away to one side as you finish to form the tail. Then pipe an adjoining round of 3cm on the opposite side to form the head, pull away to the opposite side to form the beak. Do half going one way and half the other so that they will sandwich together to form your Easter chickens for tea or pud.

3. Bake:

Aga in the simmering oven piped onto bake o glide until they come off cleanly - about 3 hours.

Electric fan oven 50 °c (Gas mark $1/4$) for 2-4 hours depending on how dried out you like your meringues.

4. Allow to cool on a cooling tray and sandwich together with whipped cream. They can be served with fresh strawberries for a dessert. The final flourish is to paint a yellow beak and a red or blue eye on the meringues!

Easter Egg Bread & Butter Pudding

If you are fed up with too many Easter eggs, use them up to make the proverbial bread and butter pudding!

Ingredients:

8-12 Rounds of bread and butter
1 Large Easter egg or150-200 gms chocolate eggs
300ml. Cream
2 Large eggs
50g. Chopped hazelnuts-optional
50g. Sultanas-optional
30g. Demerara sugar

Method:

1. Break up the Easter egg into pieces and mix with the fruit and nuts.

2. Butter a shallow ovenproof dish.

3. Arrange a single layer of bread in the dish and sprinkle over 3/4 of the chocolate,sultanas and nuts then put another layer of bread in the dish and sprinkle over the remaining chocolate mixture and the sultanas if are using them.

4. Beat together the cream and the eggs and pour it over the bread. The pudding is always better if it is left it to stand for 30 minutes before cooking. ·

5. Sprinkle over the chopped hazelnuts, this give a crunch to the top,
and cook.

Aga on the grid shelf on the floor of the roasting oven for 15-20 minutes

Electric fan oven 170°c
for 20-25 minutes
Combination oven 200°c and 180 watt for 12-15 minute

April

The month arrives with April Fools' Day (so some foolish recipes!) April is the in-between month - it tempts us with some sunshine, but it's still wet and windy enough to send us indoors to cook, play and create.
If you remembered to put your bottomless bucket over your rhubarb to encourage them to reach skywards, the first tender stalks should be shooting up. These are always so tasty. They are the first fruit out of the garden each year and there too many good recipes for them, so which should I share with you?

RECIPES

Rhubarb Fool Plus Plus

Brandysnaps

Rhubarb Summer Pudding

Rhubarb Crumble

Rhubarb Marmalade

Coffee Baked Quail

Spicy Lamb

Tiger Hunt Curry

Paratha Indian Bread

Guacamole

Avocado and Chicken Livers Salad

Chicken Liver Pâté

Thoughts on Carrots

Red Hot Bread and Butter Pudding

H.R.T. Flapjack

Sticky Toffee Pudding

Fudge Sauce

Rhubarb Fool

Rhubarb combines well with oranges, but also with ginger and cinnamon. The choice is yours - whichever one you don't like, leave it out and use an alternative!

Ingredients:

500g Rhubarb
5cm Piece root ginger
100g Sugar
200ml. Double cream

Method:

1. Wash and trim the rhubarb. Cut into 5cm pieces and place in an ovenproof dish, with a lid.

2. Peel and grate the ginger and spread over the rhubarb.

3. Sprinkle the sugar over the rhubarb. Cover and leave to stand for 30 minutes to allow the sugar to dissolve slightly.

Cook:

Aag: Place on the grid shelf on the floor of the baking oven for 20 minutes, until just soft. If it is not soft after 20 minutes, place in the simmering oven until it is.
OR in the roasting oven for 10minutes, followed by 20minutes in the simmering oven.

Electric: Cook at 150°c (Gas mark 3) for 20 minutes. Microwave 600watt for 5minutes.

OR you could stew in a saucepan on the hob with 2tbs water. Add the sugar once the rhubarb is starting to soften.

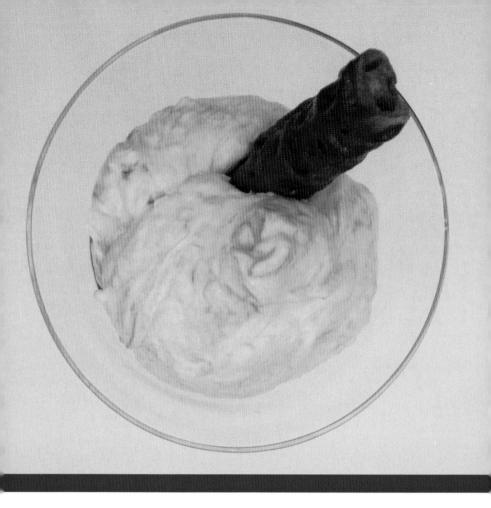

4. Allow to cool, (or serve hot with a dollop of Greek yogurt!) Whip the cream until it is just holding its shape and fold in the rhubarb.
5. Serve in individual glasses or dishes with a brandy-snap. Pop the brandy-snap in just before serving to prevent it going limp! If you want a less rich fool use 1/2 Greek yogurt or thick cold custard with 1/2 the amount of cream, fold this into the cream before adding the rhubarb.

Brandy-snaps (This makes 24 small Brandy-snaps)

Ingredients:

60g Butter
60g Castor sugar
60g Golden syrup
60g Plain flour
1tsp Ground ginger
1/2 tsp Brandy

Method:

1. Melt together the butter, sugar and golden syrup, either on the hob or in the microwave at 360watt for 2 minutes until just melted. Remove from the heat and allow to cool slightly.

2. Sieve together the flour and the ground ginger into a bowl.

3. Add the brandy and the melted ingredients to the flour bowl and beat well.

4. Line two baking sheets with bake-o-glide and place teaspoons of the mixture well apart on the sheets. This is to allow for spreading as they cook.

Cook:

Aga: On the bottom set of runners in the baking oven for 8-10minutes OR
The bottom set of runner in the roasting oven for 5-7 minutes.
Check half way through the cooking time to turn if necessary, to give an even golden brown.

Electric Fan oven 160°C
(Gas mark 5) for10 minutes.

5. As you take the first tray out of the oven, put the next tray in.

6. Allow to cool for a minute or two. Then lift them carefully off the tray with a palette knife and wrap around a buttered wooden spoon handle to form a brandy snap. Alternatively you can mold them over the bottom of a glass to form a basket.

7. Remove from the wooden spoon or glass and allow to go cold on a cooling tray. These can be kept in an airtight tin for a few days.

Rhubarb Summer Pudding

Ingredients:

500g Rhubarb
10cm Piece fresh root ginger
100g Sugar
A loaf Brioche bread OR a packet
of trifle sponges.
150ml. Double cream OR Greek
yogurt to serve

Method:

1. Wash and trim the rhubarb and
   cut into 5cm pieces. Place in an
   ovenproof dish, with a lid.

2. Peel and grate the ginger and
   spread over the rhubarb.
   Sprinkle the sugar over the
   rhubarb. Cover and stand for 30
   minutes to allow the sugar to
   dissolve slightly.

Cook

Aga: Place on the grid shelf on the
floor of the baking oven for
20 minutes until just soft. If the
rhubarb is not soft after 20 minutes,
place in the simmering oven
until it is.
OR cook in the roasting oven for 10
minutes, followed by 20 minutes in
the simmering oven.

Electric: Fan oven at 150ºc
(Gas Mark 3) for 20 minutes.
Microwave 600 watt for 5 minutes.
OR you could stew the rhubarb
in a saucepan on the hob with 2tbs
water. Add the sugar once the
rhubarb is starting to soften.

3. While the rhubarb is cooking, removing the crust from the bread and slice it. Line a pudding basin or the ramekins with slices of the brioche or the trifle sponges cut into 3 layer. If you are worried about turning it out line the base with baking parchment.

4. Stir the rhubarb to break it up and half fill the lined container. Add another layer of Brioche or trifle sponges sliced, then more rhubarb and top with a final layer of brioche or sponge.

5. If you are using a pudding bowl, cover with a small plate or saucer which fits inside the bowl. Weigh down it with a tin of something. If you are using ramekins, put a double layer of baking parchment over the top and place another ramekin with a weight in on top and chill, preferably overnight.

6. Run a knife around the edge and turn out onto a serving dish. You can pipe whipped cream over the top or serve cream separately.

Rhubarb Crumble

This is everyone's favourite crumble, even if they don't like rhubarb on its own! This is my basic crumble recipe for any fruit - you can adapt it to what is available. I do like to use butter for crumble as it gives a crispier and tastier end product. Crumble is amenable, adaptable and delicious, what more can I say!

Ingredients:

Approximately 750g Rhubarb
(Or whatever fruit you like, you could have a combination of rhubarb and mango, pear, or strawberry. These are just examples - the choice is yours!)
100g Sugar
A little root ginger grated or the grated zest and juice of an orange and the juice or 1/2tsp.ground cinnamon mixed with the sugar and/or a handful of sultanas or raisins.
The Crumble
200g Plain flour
150g Butter
75g Sugar ,Demerara or granulated give more crunch, but use what you have in stock
50g Brazil nuts chopped OR Sultanas OR Chocolate chips OR chopped dates and walnuts.

Method:

1. Prepare fruit and cut it up into uniform pieces. Put the pieces into an ovenproof dish. Mix your choice of additional flavourings with the sugar and sprinkle over the fruit.

2. Put in the oven to start cooking as you prepare the topping. Cook for about 10 minutes.

3. Rub the butter and sugar into the flour to form breadcrumbs and add the other ingredients of your choice. (Nuts, dried fruit or chocolate chips)

4. Remove the dish from the oven and sprinkle the crumble over the fruit.

To Cook

Aga: In the baking oven on the grid shelf on the floor of the oven for 30 - 40 minutes
OR in the roasting oven on the grid shelf on the floor of the oven for 20 minutes and a further 20 minutes in the simmering oven.

Electric: Fan oven 160°c (Gas mark 5) for 30-40 minutes until lightly golden brown.
Combination cooking - cook at 160°c and 360 watt for 15-20 minutes.

Rhubarb Marmalade

This is delicious with cold meat, pâtés, oily fish and sausages.

Ingredients:

200g Red onion
200g Rhubarb (OR a mixture of
rhubarb and pear)
60g Sugar
60g Butter
2cm. Piece of root ginger
3tbs Red Wine vinegar
Salt and pepper
1 Orange (optional)

Method:

1. Peel and chop the onion. Place in a heavy based saucepan with the butter and sugar. Heat gently to soften the onion.

2. Wash the rhubarb and cut up. If you are using pears, peel and chop them. Peel and grate or chop the ginger.

3. Increase the heat and when the mixture starts to colour add the rhubarb and ginger and pear, if included. Stir until the fruit starts to soften and add the wine vinegar and seasoning. Put the lid on and simmer gently until a thick marmalade. If it is too runny remove the lid and increase the heat or put on the floor of the roasting oven until it has reduced to the right texture. If you want you can add the zest of an orange and half the juice.

4. The marmalade can be served hot or cold. Remove from the heat and cool slightly before potting in a clean warm jar. Store in the refrigerator.

Coffee Baked Quail

It works! Great Colour! Interesting flavour!

Ingredients:

4 Oven ready Quail
50g Butter
1 tsp. Coffee Powder
50g Whole meal Flour
Salt and Pepper
For the sauce:
425g Tin of Tomatoes
2 Cloves garlic
Splash of Red Wine
A handful of Fresh Herbs such as
Parsley, Basil, Rosemary, or a
combination of your favourite herbs.

Method:

First make the sauce

1. Put the tomatoes, crushed or chopped garlic, herbs and wine into a saucepan and bring to the boil. Boil for 2 minutes and then place in the simmering oven for about an hour, or simmer gently on the hob.

2. Melt the butter (on the back of the Aga) with the coffee powder.

3. Brush the Quail with this mix, and then toss them in the flour, salt and pepper, in a polythene bag.

4. Place in the roasting tin; brush over with the remaining butter and cook.

Aga: Cook in the roasting oven for 15-20 minutes, until the juices run clear

Electric: Cook 170°C (Gas Mark 6) for 15-20 minutes

5. When the quail are cooked place them on top of the sauce and

keep warm until ready to serve.
If you want you can cut some new
potatoes up in 1cm slices or dice
them. Toss these in the butter
around the birds and cook with the
quail. Then you just need some
quickly cooked green vegetables for
a speedy meal, or just a salad.
Small quail can be served as a
starter on a 10cm square or circle
croûte of fried bread or toast with
salad garnish.

Spicy Lamb

This is one that needs a little forward planning! The meat develops a wonderful flavour as it marinades in Moroccan inspired spices and herbs (we use lamb instead of goat!) but the cooking is very simple.

Ingredients:

A Leg of lamb
1 Large onion
6 Large cloves of garlic
A Large handful fresh coriander (a small packet from the supermarket)
Large handful fresh parsley
2 tbs Paprika
2 tbs Ground cumin
2 tsp Cayenne pepper
The zest and rind of a lemon
3tbs Olive oil
1/2tsp. Salt

Method:

1. Wipe over the lamb and pierce the skin all over with a carving fork to make deep incisions into the meat to allow the marinade to seep in.

2. I always do this next step in the food processor. Peel and cut up the onion and place in the processor bowl. Peel the garlic, add to the bowl with the paprika, cumin, cayenne, zest and rind of the lemon and oil, and salt.

3. Wash and dry the herbs. Set the processor running and add the herbs through the feeder hole. Process until you have a well-mixed paste.

4. Place the lamb on cling film and turn the mixture onto it. Smooth the mixture all around the leg and wrap it up in cling film to absorb the flavours. Leave in the refrigerator for at least 24 hours, but preferably up to 3 days.

5. Take the lamb out of the refrigerator and allow to come back to room temperature. Remove the cling film and cook the lamb on a trivet in the roasting tin.

To Cook:

Aga: With the roasting tin on the 3rd set of runners, cook in the roasting oven for 1 hour and then in the simmering oven until tender (about 2hrs depending on the size of the leg)

Electric: Fan oven 160°c for 40 minutes per kilo plus 20 minutes.

For the last 30-40 minutes of cooking, slice 3 or 4 large onions and place in the juices underneath the rack. Stir so that they are well coated and they will cook under the lamb.

Usually this is served with rice and vegetables. The onions can be stirred in to the rice with a handful of raisins.

Tiger Hunt Curry

This is a recipe I was given whilst trying to spy a tiger in Rajhastan with Sarah, my daughter. It is for a curd cheese made with Buffalo milk which is part of the staple diet of the local Indians. They serve it curried, which is not to everyone's taste, but is interesting. We didn't find a tiger, but we saw lots of warm paw prints! We knew they were there and I think it was right that the noble beast probably lay in the bushes quietly watching us as we desperately tried to spy him! But a great holiday nevertheless, where we did spy lots of lovely people!

Ingredients:

250g Buffalo curd cheese, cut into 3 cm. cubes
2tbs Olive oil
1 Large onion
2 Cloves garlic
4 Large fresh tomatoes you could use a tin
2tsp Garam masala curry powder
OR
A little fresh red chilli pepper
A little fresh root ginger
1/4tsp Ground cloves
1/4tsp Ground nutmeg
1/4tsp Ground cinnamon
1/4tsp Cardamon
1/4tsp Ground turmeric
1/2tsp Cumin seeds
Salt and Pepper
Handful of fresh coriander

Method:

1. Peel and chop the onion and garlic. Remove the skins from the tomatoes, quarter them and remove the seeds.

2. Heat the oil in a pan. Add the onion and garlic. As they start to soften, add the curry powder, cumin seeds stirring as you add them. As their flavour is released, add the cloves, cardamon, nutmeg, cinnamon and turmeric.

3. Grate about 1/2tsp root ginger and chop finely a little chili pepper. The amount of these you use dictates the heat of the curry. Add these to the pan and the tomatoes. Stir as they start cooking. Add a little water if the sauce seems dry. Put the lid on the pan and simmer slowly for about 15 minutes.

4. Cut the cheese into about 3cm cubes. Add this to the sauce and just heat through.

5. Cut the coriander leaves into the pan with a pair of scissors. Serve on a bed of rice and Indian Paratha Bread.

Indian Bread Paratha

Makes 8-10

Ingredients:

400g Strong white bread flour
Salt
Mashed cooked potato
Fresh coriander
2 Sundried tomatoes (preserved in oil) or flavourings of your choice.
Vegetable oil
A little butter

Method:

1. Sieve the flour into a bowl. Make a well in the centre and add enough water to make a stiff dough. Cover and allow it to rest.

2. Beat the potato so that it is smooth and add cut up fresh coriander. Chop the sundried tomatoes into quite small pieces and add these. Check the seasoning.

3. Take a tablespoonful of the dough and roll it out into a circle the size of a side plate.

4. Take a large teaspoonful of the mashed potato mix and place it in the centre of the dough. Draw up the sides and seal it in, turn it over and roll carefully out into a circle.

5. Heat the oil in a frying pan and fry over quite a hot heat until it starts to bubble. Add a knob of butter to the pan. Turn the paratha over and brown the other side.
   These breads can be served with any curries.

Gaucamole

Avocados make wonderful salad bases. Their texture is a good contrast to most salad stuffs. You can make a nice light mousse which can be made with them too, but in April we've got a simple, but enjoyable Guacamole. Tomato and chilli can be added.

Ingredients:

To each avocado:
2 Cloves of garlic
The zest and juice of a lime (if they are getting a little dry use a lemon)
Salt and freshly ground pepper

Method:

Another time when the processor can do the work!

1. With a zester (a little tool I could not live without) remove the zest from the lime or lemon. A tip for getting juice out of a lime or a lemon: if you put it in the microwave for just a minute at 360 watts, this will help the juice to flow!

2. Cut the avocado in two. Remove the stone and peel off the skin. Cut the avocado up into the processor bowl and add the zest and the juice.

3. Crush the garlic and add with the salt and pepper. The beauty of making your own dips is that you are in charge of all the additives.

4. Remove from the bowl into a serving dish. Serve with batons of carrot, celery courgette pepper, in fact any vegetable.

5. As you have added the citrus juice it should keep its colour. If you are not eating it immediately cover it with cling film directly on the surface of the guacamole -this helps prevent discoloration.

6. A few chopped prawns could be stirred in to the dip with perhaps some chopped parsley, coriander or dill to ring the changes. Dips are such an easy nibble or starter and once you have made your own the variety is endless.
Serve with battons of vegetables.

Avacado Salad

Ingredients:

2 Avocados
A selection of small leaf salad,
watercress and rocket.
A few stoned green olives

The dressing:
1 Part white wine vinegar to
2 Parts olive oil or sunflower oil or a
mixture of oils
A crushed clove of garlic
Salt and pepper
1/2 tsp. Sugar
1tbs Chopped fresh parsley
1tsp. Whole grain mustard

Method:

1. To make the dressing - take a screw top jar and put all the ingredients inside. Put the lid firmly on and shake thoroughly. Taste, adjust if necessary, and put the salad together

2. Cut the avocado in half, remove the stone and the skin and cut into thick slices. Alternatively you could serve the chicken livers in the whole half. Put a little dressing on the surface of the avocado to stop discoloration.

3. Arrange a small heap of salad leaves on the plate. Slice the olives and scatter them over. Arrange the avocado slices in a circle and add a little more dressing, then pile the chicken livers in the centre or in the stone hole, if these are being added.

Chicken Livers to serve with Avacado Salad

Ingredients:

200g Chicken livers
A little milk
30g Butter
1tbs. Oil
2 Cloves garlic
2 Spring onions
1/2 A lemon
Pinch of cayenne pepper
1/2tsp.Fresh thyme
2tbs. Double cream

Method:

1. Trim any stringy bits off the livers. Cut in half if large. Put the chicken livers in a bowl and cover with milk for 5 minutes. Remove them from the bowl and dry on kitchen paper.

2. Melt the butter and oil together in a frying pan - the oil added to the butter heightens the burning point!

3. Trim and chop the spring onions. Peel and crush the garlic. Add these to the frying pan and cook gently until just softening.

4. Add the chicken livers and the thyme and cook quickly until just slightly pink in the middle.

5. Sprinkle a little cayenne pepper onto the cut surface of the lemon and give one good squeeze over the pan. At this point you could add 2 tbs brandy and set light to it! Or just stir in the cream straight away, and serve on the Avocado salad.

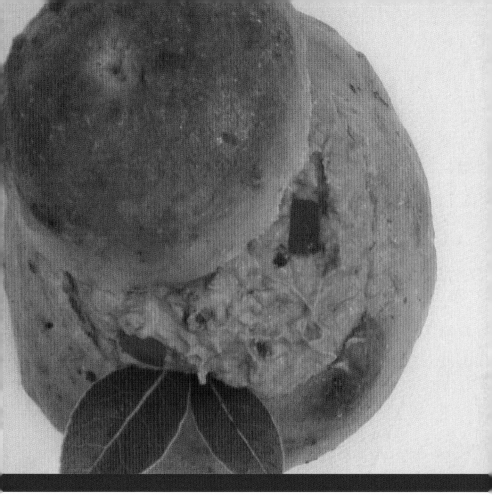

Chicken Liver Pâté

Once the chicken livers are cooked as before, you could make chicken liver pâté as follows:

1. Add another spoonful of cream and a little more butter, and put the whole lot in the food processor.

2. Process until smooth and remove from the processor. I like to add a teaspoonful or two of finely chopped red pepper and 2 tsp pink or green (wet) peppercorns at this point.

3. Stir these through and put in a dish or in individual ramekin dishes. Pour a thin layer of melted butter over the top and lay a bay leaf in the butter, or serve in a hollowed out roll as above.

These are great starters to make a few days in advance - it gives you time to make some fresh bread to serve it with! For the finishing touch serve it with the rhubarb marmalade.

Thoughts On Carrots

I think these colourful vegetables are my favourite, a few simple ways of ringing the changes with different ingredients added to the carrots:
Instead of boiling in the normal way and adding a little butter and chopped parsley.

Options:

For 500gms. Carrots

CURRIED CARROTS

Melt 50gms. butter in a saucepan add the sliced carrot and 2 chopped spring onion and sauté gently for a few minutes. You could add a teaspoon of curry powder as well, and or a clove of crushed garlic. Add a little salt , pepper and 1/2 tsp. sugar. Another addition at this stage could be 40gms. Sultanas or raisins soaked for 5mins in boiling water, drain and add to the pan, stir well, put on a well fitting lid and cook (in the oven for about 20 minutes the"AGA" way in the simmering oven) OR turn down the heat as low as possible and cook for 10 mins. check and stir and cook for a further 5 mins.until the carrots are as tender as you want them, chop some parsley or coriander stir this through and serve.

CITRUS CARROTS

OR squeeze over the juice of 1/2 a lemon or orange and serve.

YOGURTY CARROTS

OR add 100ml. Natural yogurt stir gently together , this makes it a good vegetable with sauce, when you don't want to make an extra sauce with simply cooked chops of fish.

STIR-FRY CARROTS

Stir fried carrots are good value for colour and texture, for a change peel the carrots and use a potato peeler to make ribbons going lengthways down the carrot.
Heat the wok until it is hot add 1or2 tbs oil,heat this add a little grated fresh ginger and a teaspoonful of seedy mustard, a handful of your favourite nuts,(I like cashews nuts,) and the carrot ribbons, stir quickly for 2-3 minutes and add 1tbs. Runny honey stir through and not only do they taste good they look good too! Enjoy!

Redhot Bread and Butter Pudding

Ingredients:

8-12 slices of old bread buttered
300ml. Single cream
2tbs Tomato pureè
Salt, pepper
 Tabasco sauce
2 Large eggs
1 Red onion sliced
1 Red pepper
1 Red chilli pepper
1 Jalapio pepper
2 Cloves of garlic
2tbs. Oil
100g. Mature cheese grated or
crumbled, the choice is yours

Method:

1. Wash and deseed the peppers
   and cut into fine slices.

2. Peel and slice the onion and
   the garlic.

3. Heat the oil and fry the onion,
   garlic and peppers together so
   that they take a little colour, but
   don't brown too much.

4. Butter an ovenproof dish, cut the
   slices of bread in half and line
   the dish with them butter side up
   in a single layer. Spread 3/4 of the
   pepper and onion mix over the
   bread. Add another layer of
   bread topped with the remaining
   pepper mix.
   Beat together the cream and
   eggs. Season with salt, ground
   black pepper and a dash of
   tabasco. Pour this over the
   bread mix and leave to stand for
   15 minutes before cooking
   scatter the chese over the top.

Cook

Aga: On the grid shelf on the floor of
the roasting oven for about 20
minutes. I don't like it too solid!

Electric:
Fan oven 170ºc (Gas mark 6)
for 20-25 minutes.
Combination oven 360 watt
microwave with 200ºc
for 10-12 minutes.

Just serve with a simple
cooling salad.

H.R.T. Flapjack

A far from foolish recipe. When we ladies reach a certain age our bodies' resources need a little help! The advantage of this is that the whole family likes it. I'm not sure of the effect on men - I'm working on a testosterone cake! I have several friends who find that a small piece a day helps them to keep their equilibrium. One of these is my guinea pig for this recipe - dear Barbara who keeps the mess under control in the home while I'm writing this book. She's a friend I couldn't cope without, so I have to keep her happy and well!

As with all the food we eat, reliable sources of ingredients are important. I am lucky to have Daily Bread Wholefood suppliers in Northampton not far away. They do mail order if you have problems finding dry goods. The recipe can be adapted to what is in the store cupboard. Soya, linseed and bran are the most important ingredients. With all these seeds, is it any wonder that we females are lovingly referred to as birds?!

Ingredients:

325g Soya margarine
2 tbs. Honey, golden syrup or black treacle
175g Brown sugar , I like to use demerara as it gives a nice crunch.
100g Dried fruit, Papaya or mango or cranberries
60g Linseed
60g Sunflower seed
100g Oatbran
100g Jumbo oat
200gms Rolled oats
100gms Almonds ground or finely chopped
60g Pumpkin seeds
60gSesame seeds
A good pinch of salt

Method:

1. Melt together the honey, sugar and margarine. Add the dry ingredients.
    Mix all the dry ingredients in thoroughly. Put in a large roasting tin lined with bake-o-glide, press firmly down and cook.

2. **Aga:** for 20 - 40 minutes on the bottom set of runners in the baking oven, until it is as brown as you like, depending if you like it "soggy "or really crisp.
    Or on the grid shelf on the floor of the roasting oven for 15-30 minutes. It may need turning half way and the cold shelf putting in.

    Electric: fan oven 160°c (Gas mark 5) for 25-40 minutes.

3. Allow to cool completely in the
   tin, but while it is still warm(or
   you will only have one very large
   piece!) cut it into squares with a
   blunt round bladed knife (so as
   not to damage the bake o glide).
   Remove from the tin and keep in
   an air tight tin or box.

4. If they are not eaten by passing
   family, the crumbs left in the tin
   make a very good cereal, or
   icecream topping!

Sticky Toffee Pudding

This is Tom's second favourite pudding after Baked Alaska. What can I say, this is the pud that has developed into the foolproof recipe that lots of you have enjoyed over the years at demonstrations all over the world. It was the only reason that Mike came to all my demonstrations throughout Canada and in Seattle!

Ingredients:

150g Dates
150ml. Boiling water
1/2 tps Bicarbonate of Soda
100g Butter
100g Soft Brown Sugar
150g Self Raising Flour
30 g. Fresh breadcrumbs
2 Eggs

Method:

1. Put the Dates with the Bicarbonate of Soda into a bowl and pour over the boiling water and leave to go cold.

2. Grease a pudding basin. For foolproof removal, place a small circle of bake-o-glide in the bottom of the basin.

3. Put all the ingredients in a bowl, including the dates. Beat well and pour into the pudding basin. Cover with a lid or foil or, if microwaving, cling film.

4. Bring 5cm of water to the boil in a large saucepan and place the pudding bowl in this. Put the lid on and bring back to the boil and simmer for about 2$^{1}/_{2}$ hours (this can be done in the simmering oven of the Aga - give it $^{1}/_{4}$ hour on the floor of the roasting oven first before moving it to the simmering oven).

5. If you are microwaving the pudding, put the covered bowl, (don't forget to pierce the cling) straight in the microwave and cook at 800 or 900 watt for 7-9 minutes.

6. When cooked, carefully remove the covered pudding bowl from the saucepan (or microwave) and remove the lid. Turn out on to the serving plate and serve with fudge sauce.

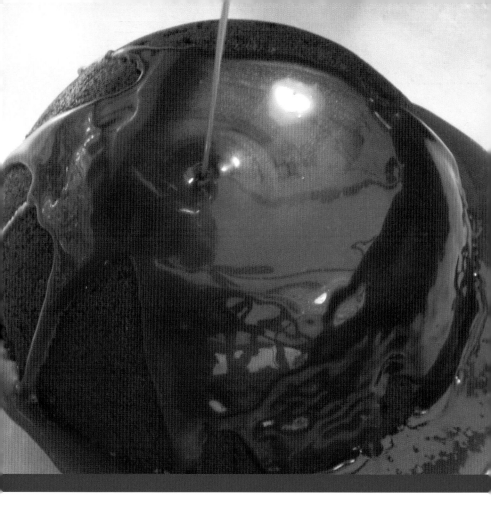

Fudge Sauce

Ingredients:

150g Soft brown sugar
100g Butter
150ml. Fresh cream
or evaporated milk

Method:

1. Place all the ingredients in an ovenproof jug and heat together gently on the back of the Aga until they are all melted or microwave 360 watt for 4 minutes.

2. Take a hand whisk and whisk until you have a smooth fudge sauce. (This sauce is equally delicious poured over ice cream,) but pour some over the Sticky Toffee Pudding and serve the rest separately.
   Enjoy all those lovely calories!

May

Asparagus is so good when you can pick it up freshly cut from the asparagus beds. Rinse it and cook it quickly for just two minutes in boiling salted water. Serve with melted butter and a squeeze of lemon juice. New Potatoes, Jersey Royals, really wee ones, tossed in a dressing with fresh garden mint and some asparagus and baby carrots makes a meal in itself. Lots of vegetables are the ideal diet as summer approaches and we need to shed a pound or two for the bikini to fit!

RECIPES

Thoughts on ASPARAGUS

Hollandaise Sauce

Filo Fish tartlets

Asparagus bread and butter pudding

Basic Risotto

Stuffed leg of Spring lamb

Dandelion salad

Guinea fowl stir-fry

Savarin or Rum Baba

Passion fruit soufflé

Viennese kisses or fingers

Bounty cake

Asparagus

How to cook?

Trim the spears to an even length - you can use the end of the stalks to make soup. Rinse the spears well in a colander and steam for 4-6 minutes or microwave.

To microwave: Arrange tips to the centre of the dish. Cover and microwave 450g of asparagus for 5-7 mins at 600 watts and allow to stand for 2-3 minutes.

Asparagus Pan

The principle of the asparagus pan is the stalks are in the water and the tips steam. You can make your own, using an empty tin from which you have removed both ends, so that you have a collar to stand in the saucepan. Put the asparagus in and make a lid with a piece of foil, tented over the top. Simmer gently for 4-5 minutes.

Saucepan

I just use a saucepan, big enough to lay the spears in. Bring the salted water to the boil, add the asparagus and cook it quickly for 2 minutes. Drain it and serve. I like it still with bite, it also preserves the colour, which is so fresh.

Chargrilled Asparagus

Brush the raw asparagus with a little oil - nutty ones are good - and cook on a well heated grill pan. Cook for a couple of minutes on each side so that you have lovely chargrilled lines all round.

Battered Asparagus

Make a batter with self-raising flour and tonic water. Season with salt and pepper. Coat the asparagus spears and deep fat fry for 3 minutes and drain well on kitchen paper.

Once you have cooked the asparagus, to serve with it:
Melted butter and lemon OR lime OR orange zest and juice.

Or With a fruity Hollandaise Sauce

Ingredients:

2 Egg yolks
150g Butter
Zest and juice of a lemon OR lime
OR orange
Salt and pepper if liked

Method:

1. Put the juice in a small saucepan with 1 tbs water and reduce by a tablespoonful.

2. Put the egg yolks in the small bowl of a processor and run so that the yolks blend and start to thicken. With the processor motor still running pour over the juice and run for a moment.

3. Melt the butter in the saucepan to a bubbling boil. With the processor motor running, very slowly add the butter and this will cook and thicken the eggs.

4. Scrape the sauce out of the bowl into a serving jug and check the seasoning.

5. This is the easiest hollandaise I know. You can throw a handful of herbs in while it is still in the processor and it will be chopped as it flavours the sauce. My favourites are coriander or dill.

6. A tablespoon of raspberry puree or vinegar added to a lemon hollandaise makes a subtle, pretty pink sauce.

Other Suggestions

Sauté a few spring onions and chopped mushrooms in a little oil and butter. Then add some fresh breadcrumbs and fry until crisp. Add some grated cheese and chopped nuts, e.g. walnuts, and sprinkle over freshly cooked asparagus.

Added to freshly cooked pasta with pesto and Parmesan.

Cold asparagus compliments any salads, rice or pasta, or on it's own with French dressing.

Filo Fish Tartlets

A simple starter. The tartlets can be filled with what ever is in the refrigerator and mayonnaise can replace the créme fraîche

Ingredients:

450g Asparagus
A small tub Crème Fraîche
Chives & Dill - chopped
225g Smoked Trout/Smoked
Salmon or cold cooked fresh
salmon or trout
1 Lime - sliced
36 x 10cm Squares of Filo Pastry
2tbs Melted Butter
Poppy Seeds

Method:

1. Melt the butter and arrange layers of Filo Pastry in bun tins. Brush each layer with butter. Use 3 layers per tartlet.
   Sprinkle the top layer with Poppy Seeds and cook.

Aga: in the roasting oven for 5 minutes

Electric: Fan oven 170°c (Gas mark 6) for 5 -8 minute

3. Cook the Asparagus quickly in boiling salted water for 2 minutes. Drain and cut into bite size pieces.

4. Place 2 or 3 pieces of Asparagus in each tartlet. Top this with Crème Fraîche and decorate with herbs. If using the trout or smoked salmon, twist a couple of small strips on top and garnish with herbs and the zest or a thin slice of lime.

Asparagus Bread and Butter Pudding

Ingredients:

8-12 Rounds bread and butter
300g Asparagus spears
150gms Parmesan cheese
6 Spring onions
1 or 2 cloves garlic
300ml. Cream
2 large eggs
Salt and pepper
Grated nutmeg
Optional:
A handful of walnut pieces

Method:

1. Cook the asparagus for just 3 minutes in boiling salted water. Chop and sauté the onions and the garlic in a little oil until just softened.

2. Line a buttered ovenproof dish with the bread and butter. Add a layer of asparagus and the onion mix. Cover with shavings of parmesan (shavings can be done with the potato peeler.) Season and put another layer of bread and butter and the remaining vegetables on top. Finish off with more parmesan and the walnuts if you want to include them.

3. Whisk together the cream and the eggs and pour over the other ingredients in the dish. Allow to stand for at least 1/2 an hour. Grate over a little nutmeg and cook. Until lightly golden brown with crispy edges and still a slightly soft centre.

Serve with a good crisp well-dressed salad.

To Cook:

Aga: Cook on the grid shelf on the floor of the roasting oven for 20 minutes

Electric: Fan fan oven 170ºc (Gas mark 6) for 20 - 30 mins Combination oven cook at 200ºc with 360 watt microwave for 10 - 15 mins

Basic Risotto

You have all shared this recipe with me at demonstrations and been converted to risotto fans.

Risotto is surrounded by mystery - there are orders to stir constantly, adding stock slowly, etc. It is very gentle all around heat that is necessary - the Aga is perfect for this, or a very controllable hob such as induction. This basic recipe can be adapted to individual tastes. You can add your own choice of extras to make it a starter or a filling main dish, which needs just a salad at the side.

Ingredients:

1 tbs. Oil
50g Butter
1 Medium onion- chopped, I do like the flavour of red onions
2 Cloves garlic
140 gms Risotto rice e.g. Carnaroli or Arboria
1/2 Glass white wine or about 3tbs. Dry sherry
600ml. Good vegetable stock
40g Butter or 3tbs. Of cream
Freshly grated or shaved Parmesan
Chopped or cut fresh herbs.
A selection of vegetables e.g. Surprise-asparagus, baby carrots, sugar snap peas, wild and exotic or just ordinary mushrooms!

Method:

1. Melt the oil and butter together in a large saucepan and sauté the onion and garlic until soft.

2. Add the rice and cook until transparent. Add the wine and allow to reduce. Then add all the stock, bring to the boil, stirring well. Put on a well fitting lid and put in the simmering oven of the Aga or turn down the heat so the the rice is barely moving, (induction setting 2) and let it cook for 20 minutes. After 20 minutes the stock will have been absorbed and the rice should be soft and creamy. It may need a little more cooking - brown rice takes about 30 minutes.

3. In the meantime, if using mushrooms put the mushrooms in a dish with a little oil or some of the extra butter that is to go in at the end. Pop them in the oven for 15 minutes or sauté them in a small pan on the hob. Cook the vegetables in lightly salted water for just 2 mins and drain and keep warm (save the water just in case you need any more liquid).

4. Once the rice is cooked, and the grains are plump add the extra butter or cream not essential but nice and a tablespoon of parmesan to the rice. Stir in the cooked vegetables and some herbs. Serve on a platter with the cooked mushrooms on top and extra chopped herbs, also some extra parmesan.

To the basic risotto you can add fish, or ham, chicken or smoked salmon at the end - the choice is yours. I prefer to cook the vegetables separately as this gives a better contrast of texture and you don't end up with a nasty grey mushroom risotto. Alternatively you can stir fry the vegetables instead of boiling them.

I think this serves four but my son doubles the quantities (he has a good appetite)

Stuffed Leg of Spring Lamb

Ingredients:

A Leg of lamb, ask your butcher to bone it for you
4 Slices bread
6-8 Dried apricots-soaked
A small onion or 4 Spring onions
2 tbs. Chopped mint OR 1 tbs. chopped rosemary
An orange
 Salt and pepper
OPTIONAL
1 tbs. Chopped almonds OR pecan nuts.
30 g Butter or 2tbs Oil
String, ask your butcher for some!

Method:

1. Sauté the onions until they are soft. (If you like curry a teaspoon or two of curry powder could be added to the onion as it sautés)

2. In the processor make the bread into crumbs. Add the apricots, herbs, nuts and seasoning and whiz. Add the sautéed onion with the remaining oil and the zest and juice of the orange and process to form a stuffing.

3. Open out the leg of lamb, skin side down, where the bone has been removed from, put the stuffing in the middle, draw up the sides and tie up with the string. Do not tie too tightly or it will ooze out - try and make a cushion of it (see pictures).

4. Place on a wire rack in a roasting tin and stud with garlic and rosemary if you like. You can just season it with salt and pepper.

5. Weigh the joint when it is stuffed and calculate the cooking time for the whole weight at 45 minutes per kilo plus 20 minutes.

Cook **Aga** in the roasting oven

Electric fan oven 160°c
(Gas mark 5)

6. At the end of the cooking time remove from the oven and allow the joint to rest while you make the gravy with the juices and sediment from the tin.

Making the gravy: Add some water, or for special occasions 1/2 a glass of wine, to the pan and scrape the lovely meaty sediment off the bottom of the pan. Pour it into a saucepan - the one used for the vegetables is fine - having saved the vegetable water for the gravy. To every 200ml of liquid add 1 rounded teaspoonful of cornflour. A tbs of apricot jam could be added to the gravy for the lamb.

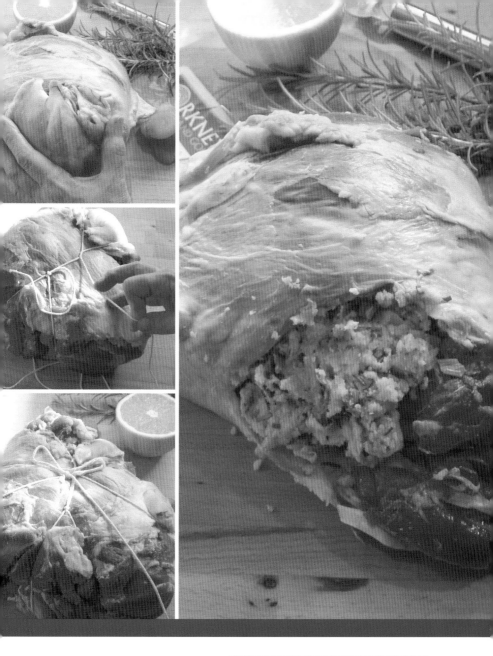

7. Taste and adjust the seasoning for the gravy and serve with the lamb with some minted Jersey Royal new potatoes, simple baby carrots and Spring cabbage or any other green vegetable.

Dandelion Salad

A very seasonal salad, which is very popular on the Continent. This can also be made with other small salad leaves. Some garlic can be added to the bacon as it cooks.

Ingredients:

500g Dandelion leaves
200 g Streaky bacon
French Dressing:-
3 parts oil
1 part wine vinegar
Salt
Pepper
A little mustard
Crushed garlic
1/2 tsp. Caster sugar

Method:

1. Wash the dandelion leaves really thoroughly and dry.

2. Cut the bacon up into small pieces and fry in their own fat until crisp and toss with the leaves with about 4 tbs of dressing and serve straight away.

3. Instead of bacon you could add some croûtons of fried or dried bread with some Parmesan shavings and nuts.

4. Place all the dressing ingredients in a screw top jar and shake thoroughly!

   I have not included many salads as they are on television every day! A good imagination can throw a salad together in no time!

Guineas Fowl Stir-Fry

Ingredients:

350g Boneless Guinea Fowl breast cut into bite size pieces or strips
Salt and Pepper
3tbs Oil
1-2 tsp. Grated Root Ginger
1 Red Pepper cut into slices
3 Mushrooms Sliced
3 Spring onions chopped
Rind of 1/2 Orange
2 tbs. Dry Sherry
1/2 tsp. Sugar
1/2 tsp. Cornflour
1 tbs. Soy Sauce
1 tbs.Orange Juice
1/2 a Ripe mango optional
2tbs. Flaked toasted almonds

Method:

1. Season the meat and toss with 2tbs oil (this can be done in a polythene bag).

2. Heat the wok and add the remaining oil. Add the guinea fowl and cook for 2 minutes.

3. Add the ginger, pepper and mushrooms and cook for a further minute, add the orange rind and spring onions.

4. If you are using mango you should at this point add the chopped mango - you will need 1/2 a mango for this amount of Guinea Fowl.

5. Cook for a further minute and mix the cornflour with the sherry and soy sauce. Add this and stir-fry for a further minute.

6. Transfer to a warm plate and sprinkle with orange juice and flaked almonds.

7. This can be served on a bed of rice.

Savarin or Rum Baba

There is something very satisfying about yeast recipes. This is good because it doesn't leave you with mountains of dough. The basic savarin is an ideal way of using fresh cherries as they are just appearing on the shelves, (or tree!) but the choice of fruit is yours.

Ingredients:

140g Strong white Bread Flour
A pinch of salt
7g Dried yeast, one packet.
20g Caster Sugar
50g Butter
2 Eggs
60ml. Warm milk
Syrup:
200g Granulated sugar
200ml. Water
A split vanilla pod
Kirsch, sherry, brandy, rum or your favourite liqueur-about 6 tbs
100g Blanched almonds
500g Fresh fruit

Method:

1. Sieve the flour in a bowl with the salt and put to warm.

2. Melt the butter. Add the milk and sprinkle over the yeast. Whisk together, then pour over the flour and leave in a warm place to "sponge"for 30 minutes i.e. on the top of the Aga with a chefs pad underneath or if you have an oven with a bread proving function use this. Or in the airing cupboard!

3. Put the water and sugar in a saucepan with the split vanilla pod and bring to the boil. Boil for 5 minutes and remove from the heat and allow to cool. Take out the vanilla pod and then, if you want to, add the alcohol of your choice. This is not essential as you have a delicious vanilla syrup.

4. After the Savarin mixture has sponged, beat together the eggs. Add these and beat it all to a smooth dough. This can take about 5 minutes by hand or you can use an electric mixer - but hand beating is quite therapeutic if you've had a bad day! If you are making a Rum Baba add a handful of currants or sultanas to the dough as you finish mixing, but not before as the currents could disintegrate.

5. Butter a ring mould tin and base line it with baking parchment, if you are worried about turning it out. Pour the dough into the tin, but don't more than half fill it. Put it to prove in a warm place again - not too hot, the yeast is killed off at 40°c and would not rise!

When it has doubled in bulk, usually after about 30 minutes, it is ready.

To cook:

Aga: In the roasting oven on the grid shelf for 10 minutes and then for 20 more minutes in the baking oven. Alternatively you can put the cold shelf above as it in the roasting oven and cook it for 15-20 minutes more there.

Electric: Fan oven 200°c (Gas mark 8) for 10 mins and then reduce the temperature to160°c (Gas mark 5) for a futher 20-30 minutes until it is a golden brown.

6. Invert the savarin onto a cooling rack. After 10 minutes loosen the edges and turn out.

7. While it is still warm put on the serving plate. Spike with a skewer and spoon over the syrup. Keep a little back to pour over just before eating.

8. Prepare the fruit: wash and dry it and if there are stones remove them. Pile the fruit in the centre, and spike with the blanched almonds.It can be served with cream or Greek yogurt.

Passion Fruit Soufflé

A good basic soufflè recipe which can be adapted to any fruit within reason. I have loved passion fruit since a visit to New Zealand, where they appear on every menu, in lots of guises. You can substitute them for lemon in many recipes, give them a try! If you need praline the recipe is October.

Ingredients:

4 Passion fruit
150g Caster sugar
3 Eggs
1 Level dessertspoon powdered gelatine
3 tbs. Water
240ml. Double cream for the soufflé and a little extra to decorate
4 Passion fruit for sauce
A tbs Clear honey
A few chopped nuts or some praline

Method:

1. Put the water into a ramekin dish and sprinkle over the gelatine and put it on the back of the Aga to melt or in the microwave at 360watt for 1 minutes stir and allow to cool slightly.

2. Separate the eggs .

3. Whisk the egg yolks with the sugar until thick and creamy.

4. Cut the passion fruit in half and scoop out the seeds into the bowl of the food processor and run until the juice runs freely.

Put through a sieve to remove the seeds and add the juice slowly to the yolk mix, whisking all the time.

5. Whip the cream to "soft peaks"

6. Whisk the egg whites also to "soft peaks", but not dry.

7. Add the gelatine to the yolk mixture, mixing thoroughly but gently and then fold in the cream.

8. Fold 2tbs egg white into the other mixture. Then add this gently to the rest of the egg white. You will find that they will blend together far more easily if you add the small amount of egg white first.
Whenever mixing two mixtures of different textures together add a little of the lighter one to the heavier one first.

9. Put the mixture in the soufflé dish to set. If you want the soufflé to stand up above the dish tie a collar of double baking parchment or even bake-o-glide round the top of the dish to stand 6-8 cm above the rim of

the dish - a 900ml capacity dish is suitable for this amount. Alternatively spoon into individual ramekin dishes (6-8 dishes) and allow to set.

10. When set, carefully remove the collar and press some chopped nuts, pistachio look so pretty or praline powder onto the edges above the rim. Decorate with whipped cream and some Lavender flowers if you have any in the garden or any pretty little flower as long as it isn't poisonous!

11. For the sauce, treat the other 4 passion fruits in the same way, but it is not necessary to sieve the sauce - the seeds look quite attractive. Whizz the honey with the pulp to sweeten it and serve separately, or just pour a little on the top of the soufflés in the ramekins. As you put the soufflé mixture in the ramekins you can pour a tablespoon of the sauce through the mixture to give a rippled effect.

Serve with Viennese finger, this compliments the texture of the soufflé.

Viennese Kisses or Fingers

Ingredients:

200g Butter
60g Icing Sugar
1/2 tsp Vanilla Essence
200g Plain flour
Halved glacé cherries
Chocolate to melt

Method:

1. Put the chocolate to melt on the back of the Aga

2. Cream the butter, sugar and vanilla essence until really light and creamy.

3. Fold the flour in carefully to give a soft dough.

4. Place in a piping bag with a vegetable star pipe and pipe into rosettes or fingers on a baking tray lined with baking parchment or bake-o-glide. If you do rosettes you can put a small piece of glace cherry in the centre.

5. Bake and then allow to cool. Dredge the cherry whirls with icing sugar and dip the ends of the fingers into the melted chocolate. They may be sandwiched together with butter cream if desired.

To Cook:

Aga: In the baking oven on the grid shelf or the floor of the oven for 15-20 minutes until firm and very lightly golden.

Electric fan oven 170°c
(Gas mark 6) for 15 -20 minutes

Bounty Cake

Ingredients:
Cake mix:
100g S.R. Flour
120g Caster sugar
120 g Soft margarine
20g Cocoa powder
2 Large eggs

Coconut filling mix:
1 Large egg white
60 g Caster sugar
80g Desiccated coconut
20gms Plain flour

Topping:
200gms Chocolate
40gms Butter
2tbs. Water

Method:

1. Grease a 24cm diameter ring mould, and line with strips of baking parchment to ensure easy removal.

2. Place all the cake ingredients in a large bowl and beat well until light and fluffy and then put in the ring mould.

3. Beat the egg white until stiff. Add the sugar and beat again. Fold in the coconut and flour.

4. Put the mixture in a piping bag without a nozzle and pipe a circle on to the cake mix. This will sink into the cake as it cooks and create the bounty filling! It can be spooned around.

5. Bake the cake.

Aga: In the baking oven for 30- 40 minutes on the grid shelf on the bottom set of runners, or in the cake baker for 40 mins or on the grid shelf on the floor of the roasting oven with the cold shelf going in after 15 mins. Total cooking time should be about 30 minutes, until the cake is firm to the finger test.

Electric: Fan oven at 160ºc (Gas mark 5) for 30-40 minutes Combination oven - cook at 180ºC with 180 watt microwave for about 18 minutes.

6. Allow to cool in the tin for 10 minutes and then turn out and cover with the topping when the cake is cold.

7. Put all the topping ingredients in heatproof bowl melt on the back of the Aga, or in the microwave on 360 watt for 3-4 minutes Or over a pan of hot water. When it is melted whisk gently until you have a smooth chocolate topping.

8. With a plate underneath the cooling rack carfully pour and spread the chocolate over the cake and allow to set-Paradise!

June

Sunshine, light, warm, white and lovely!

RECIPES

Cucumber Ring Mousse

Three C Quiche

Stuffed Salmon

Beef Stroganoff

Watercress Roulade

Meringue Roulade

Fruity Curds

Nectarine, or Peach Bread and Butter Pudding

Earl Grey Tea bread

Kiwi Krisps

Ice creams

Sorbet

Elderflower Champagne

Cucumber Ring Mousse

Ingredients:

2 Cucumbers
2 tbs. Salt
15 gms. (Or a packet) of gelatine
250 ml. Water
Juice of $1/2$ a lemon
2 tbs. White wine vinegar
2 tsps. Caster sugar
300 gms. Cottage cheese or cream cheese
1 tbs. Cut up dill
2 Spring onions finely chopped or chives
$1/4$ tsp. Cayenne pepper
100 ml. Whipping cream
Salt to taste if necessary
A bunch of watercress

Method:

1. Oil a 1400ml ring mould.

2. Peel and dice $1 1/2$ of the cucumbers. Place in a colander and sprinkle with the salt. Leave for at least an hour - this helps to remove excess water from the cucumber, and remove any bitterness.

3. Pour the water into a bowl, sprinkle over the gelatine and leave to sponge for 5 minutes.

4. Add the vinegar, lemon juice and sugar and gently heat on the back of the Aga, over hot water in a saucepan or in the microwave at 360 watt for 2 minutes.

5. Stir and allow to cool slightly so that it is not too hot as it is added to the cheesy mix.

6. Rinse the cubed cucumber and dry on a clean tea towel. Slice the remaining cucumber thinly and arrange it in the base of the ring mould, dipping each slice in the gelatine liquid as you place them in the mould.

7. Spoon just 2 tablespoons of the gelatine over the arranged cucumber and place in the refrigerator or on a bed of ice to set.

8. Place the cottage cheese in the food processor and pulse to make it smooth. Add the herbs, onion, cayenne and the cooled but still liquid gelatine and just pulse until mixed through.

9. Remove from the processor and fold in the diced cucumber. Check the seasoning.

10. Whip the cream until it is just holding its shape and fold it into the cucumber mixture. Carefully place it in the mould and refrigerate to set, preferably overnight.

11. Dip the mould very quickly in a sink of hot water for no more than 10 seconds to loosen the mousse, draw the mousse away from the edges, turn out onto a plate and fill the centre with watercress to serve with freshly baked bread.

There is a wonderful range of packeted bread mixes that are very easy to use, and only need water or water and oil added. They are well worth having one or two in the store cupboard to try. As it smells delicious as it bakes and is very moreish!

The Three "C" Quiche

Carrot, Cheese and Coriander

This is my favourite quiche and is one of the most popular recipes at demonstrations. This is great as a starter, light lunch or picnic fodder. The pastry and filling cook at the same time. Y-Fenni is a really tasty cheese, which I use for cooking often as it has mustard seeds and ale in it and has a lovely rounded flavour. If you can't get Y-Fenni then use mature Cheddar and add 2 tsp whole grain mustard to the cream and eggs yourself. Y-Fenni is Welsh for Abergavenny and that is where it is made!

Ingredients:

500g Cooked sliced carrots
1 Packet fresh coriander
200 -300g. Y-Fenni cheese
2 Large eggs
300ml Single cream
Salt, pepper and nutmeg
A 24cm flan tin or dish lined with uncooked cheese pastry

Method:

1. Spread half the cheese over the bottom of the flan case, then the carrots, then snip the coriander with scissors over the top. Finally add a top layer of cheese and season with a little salt and freshly ground pepper.

   Beat together the eggs with the cream, pour over the filling and sprinkle some grated nutmeg on top.

2. Cook:
   Aga on the floor of the roasting oven for 20- 40 minutes.

   Electric fan oven Cook at 170°c (Gas mark 6) for 30-45 minutes on a baking sheet.

   Put the baking sheet in the oven to heat up while you are making the filling to help cook the base of the quiche.

   If you have an oven with bottom heat, cook it on this function at 200°c for 40-45 minutes, until the pastry is browned and the filling is set and lightly coloured.

3. To serve, remove the quiche from the flan tin if using a flan tin, or serve it straight from the dish if it is a ceramic flan dish.
   Serve with a watercress and coriander, dressed salad.

Cheese Pastry
Ingredients:

350g Plain flour
200g Butter
1 tsp. Dry mustard powder
1/4 tsp. Cayenne pepper
100g Mature cheese finely grated
1 Egg yolk made up to 50ml.
with water

Method:

1. Place the flour and cut up butter in the food processor and process to fine breadcrumbs.

2. Add the cheese, mustard and cayenne, pulse and then add the yolk and water with the motor running until it starts to form a ball.

3. Remove from the bowl and knead gently to a smooth ball.

4. Chill, covered, for at least 1/2hour before rolling out to line the flan dish or tin (approx. 25 cm diameter).

Stuffed Salmon

Salmon is the most adaptable of fish - it is readily available at your local supermarket and can be enjoyed by most people all the year round. The wild or the organic salmon do have more flavour and are best cooked very simply so that you can savour their delicate flavour. For this recipe we are adding flavour with lots of herbs so the farmed salmon is fine. This is a recipe I love doing at demonstrations, where it is always popular.

Make a friend of your fishmonger and he will advise you of good fish to try for a change - it's always worth trying them once! Douglas, my fishmonger is very kind and knows when I ask for a whole salmon, that my next request will be could he please fillet it for me. He always does this with a smile - thank you Douglas! The recipe is for a whole salmon but you can buy fillets and sandwich them together with the stuffing. The salmon is not covered as it is an oily fish and the flavour just intensifies as it cooks. It is also not in the oven long enough to dry out (unless you forget to put the timer on!). Salmon does vary in thickness so the timing is not always exact.

Ingredients:

1 Whole salmon filleted
6 Slices of fresh bread
15 g Fresh dill
20g Fresh coriander
2 Spring onions
50 g Hard butter, cut into small dice
Zest and juice of an orange, lemon
or 2 limes

Method:

1. Process the breadcrumbs. Cut up spring onions. Add these and the herbs to the breadcrumbs and whiz.

2. Take the lid off and add the cut up butter pieces and the zest and juice of your choice of citrus fruit (or even a mixture). Add salt and a generous twist of black pepper. Put the lid back on and process until it binds together.

3. Lay out one fillet skin side down and spread the stuffing along the fish. (Have the stuffing layer thicker at the thin end of the fillet so that it cooks more evenly.) Place the other fillet on top and lift onto a grill rack to cook. There is no need to tie it, as I have said many times in demonstrations, it isn't going anywhere, apart from onto a serving dish!

4. Cook:

   Aga in the roasting oven for
   20 minutes per kilo in the lined
   roasting tin, hanging on the 3rd
   set of runners.
   Alternatively cook in the baking
   oven for 25 minutes per kilo on
   the second set of runners - this
   gives a softer, less crispy finish.

   Electric fan oven at 160°C (Gas
   mark 5) for 25 minutes per kilo
   on the grill rack over the
   roasting tin.
   Combination oven at 180°c
   with 180 watt microwave
   for 18 minutes per kilo.

5. Take from the oven and allow to
   rest for a few moments. Remove
   the top skin, place the serving
   dish on top and turn over to
   leave the salmon on the plate as
   you turn it back. Remove the
   skin and decorate with fresh
   herbs, a sea of dill looks pretty!
   Serve with a Hollandaise sauce
   flavoured with the herbs and
   citrus fruit that are used in the
   stuffing (see May for recipe). Or
   make a rich white sauce, with
   milk infused with the herbs, a little
   of the peel of the chosen fruit,
   onion, mace and peppercorns.
   Strain the milk, make the sauce
   and flavour it with more zest and
   juice to give a delicate fruity
   sauce with which you can coat
   the salmon with a thin layer, and
   then serve the rest in a
   sauceboat separately.

   Serve with little Jersey Royal new
   potatoes and asparagus for the
   Perfect Summer supper.

Beef Stroganoff

This is really a book of my old recipes and this recipe has been there longer than any other. It adapts to the quality of the meat quite happily and is always moreish. It is best served with simple rice and a green salad, so you don't have to spend hours in the kitchen. Throw it all together and then have a quiet sit-down in the garden while the oven does the work! The simmering oven of the Aga is ideal for cooking this dish slowly or an induction hob on almost the lowest setting so that it barely moves.

Ingredients:

1 kg Good braising steak
2 Large onions
450g Mushrooms
70g Butter
1 tbs Oil
1 tbs Plain flour
Salt and pepper
1 tsp Sugar
1 tbs Tomato puree
300ml. Beef stock
200ml Soured cream
2 tbs Chopped parsley

Method:

1. Trim the beef and cut into long thin strips. Peel and slice the onions into rings.

2. Melt the butter and oil together and fry the meat and onion so that they start to brown.

3. Add the salt and pepper, sprinkle over the flour and stir well. Add the tomato puree, sugar and stock, bring to the boil and then simmer gently until tender for 1/2-1 1/2 hours depending on the cut of beef!

4. Aga in the simmering oven Electric fan oven 150°c (Gas mark 3) Or on the hob at a low setting.

5. 15 minutes before the end of the cooking time, peel and quarter the mushrooms and add them to the stroganoff.

6. Remove from the oven and stir in 1/2 of the soured cream. Place on a bed of rice, swirl over the rest of the cream and sprinkle over a generous amount of chopped parsley. Serve with a side salad.

Oven cooked rice

Oven rice is the best way of cooking rice. To each cup of well rinsed rice add 1 1/2 -2 cups of water, with a little salt. Once it has come to the boil, cover with a well fitting lid and cook in the simmering oven for 20-40 minutes depending on the type of rice you like to use - brown rice takes longest.

If using an electric fan oven cook at 150°c (Gas mark 3) for 20 - 40 minutes.

Watercress Roulade

This recipe is the basis for lots of variations - a starter, light lunch, supper or an easy vegetarian alternative. The last chance to have filling of home grown asparagus is this month, as cutting usually ends on Midsummer Day. After then you can turn to other fresh vegetables or dried fruits with olives and onions for fillings- let your imagination roll!

Ingredients:

4 Eggs
2 Packets of watercress
Salt, pepper and grated nutmeg
2 tbs. Sesame seeds

Filling:

300g Cream cheese
100 ml. Crème fraîche
100g Chopped almonds- toasted
400g Asparagus
4 Spring onions
40g Raisins
Juice of 1/2 orange

Method:

1. Line a small shallow baking tray with bake-o-glide. Separate the eggs and lightly beat the egg yolks.

2. Wash, dry and chop the watercress add to the egg yolks. Season with salt and pepper. I'm a bit of a nutmeg freak and I would add some grated nutmeg too!

3. Whisk the egg whites until stiff but not dry and fold 2 tablespoons of the egg whites into the watercress mixture. Fold it all gently together and carefully spread it in the lined tin.

4. Sprinkle over the sesame seeds and cook.

   Aga in the roasting oven on the bottom set of runners for 10 minutes.

   Electric the fan oven at 150°c (Gas mark 3) for 15 minutes.

5. Remove from the oven and leave to go cold in the tin.

6. Squeeze the orange juice over the raisins to allow them to plump up - Lexia raisins are the biggest and juiciest if you can get them.

7. Prepare the vegetables - wash, trim and cut up the spring onions into 2cm lengths. Cut the tips and some stalk off the asparagus. Cut the rest into 2cm lengths too and blanche for just 2-3 minutes. Rinse under cold water and let them go completely cold.

8. Chop the almonds. Brown them under a hot grill or in a hot oven, stirring occasionally. Let them go cold.

9. Cream the cream cheese to soften it and carefully add all the other ingredients. If the cream cheese is too stiff then add all the orange juice with the raisins. If not drain the raisins from the juice before adding them.

10. Cover the roulade in the tin with cling film and seal it in the tin and turn it over onto the work surface, lift off the tin and peel off the lining paper.

11. Spread the filling gently over the roulade, not quite to the edges as it will spread a little as you roll it up. Make a crease along the long edge with the back of a knife to help the first fold and with the help of the cling film roll up the roulade and lift on to the serving dish. Easy peasy!

See Swiss Roll in November for pictures.

Meringue Roulade

OK, roulades have been done to death, but it is such a good way to serve summer fruits. If using strawberries, wash and slice, sprinkle over a little sugar and about 3cm of grated root ginger OR balsamic vinegar OR the zest and juice of an orange and let them marinade for a while before lifting with a slotted spoon onto the cream. This recipe looks impressive and is so easy - well the way I roll them up it is, anyway! It's a real perennial. If two strapping Welsh rugby players can do this at the Royal Welsh Show after seeing me do it once then I'm sure you can!

Ingredients:

6 Very large egg whites or 7-8 smaller ones
170g Caster sugar
2tsp Cornflour

Filling:

500ml Double cream
4tbs. Lme curd (see next recipe)
OR about 200g of soft fruits
Icing sugar to dredge

Method:

1. Line a large shallow baking tray or roasting tin with non-stick parchment or bake-o-glide.

2. Whisk the egg whites until stiff. Mix the sugar and the cornflour togetherand add the sugar in three lots to the egg whites whisking well between each addition.

3. Spread carefully into the tin.

4. To Cook :
   Aga in the baking oven on the bottom set of runners for 20-30 minutes until lightly browned and bouncy to the touch.
   Alternatively cook in the roasting oven on the grid shelf for 5 minutes and then in the simmering oven for a further 15-20 minutes.

   Electric fan oven 160 °c (Gas mark 4) for 15 mins.

5. Remove from the oven and leave to go cold.

6. Dredge the meringue with icing sugar. Cover with a large piece of cling film over the top and over the edges to hold the meringue in as you turn it over.

7. Turn the meringue out on to the cling film on the work surface and peel off the baking parchment.

8. Whip the cream and fold in the curd if using this filling. Spread it carefully over the meringue, or just spread over the cream and scatter the fruit over.

9. Make an indentation with the back of the knife along the long edge and roll it up with the help of the cling film just like a Swiss roll!

10. Place on the serving dish and decorate with fruit or pretty little flowers from the garden. Check they are not poisonous, just in case anyone decides to eat them!

Fruity Curds

We are all familiar with lemon curd but you can use other fruits to ring the changes. A mixture of citrus fruits works well - if there is a lot of juice you may need an extra egg yolk. Here's a useful tip - to loosen the juice in the citrus fruits place them in the microwave for a minute at 360 watt.

500g of fruit cooked in its own juice and made into a sieved puree can be substituted for the 3 lemons if you like. The possibilities are endless!

Lime, Lemon (or both!) Curd.

Ingredients:

250 gms. Caster sugar
125 gms. Butter
Rind and juices of three citrus fruits
3 Eggs (or the yolks left over from making the meringue roulade)

Method:

1. Place butter, sugar and fruit rind and juice into a large bowl and melt together. If you have an **Aga** do this over a saucepan of simmering water on the simmering plate. Alternatively in a microwave oven at 650 watt for 3 minutes.

2. Stir well and strain in the beaten eggs. Continue to cook.

3. If using an Aga, stir over the pan of simmering water until the curd thickens.

4. In the microwave, cook at 360 watt for 1 minute. Stir and then cook for 30 seconds at a time until a creamy curd is made.

5. Pot and cover. Keep refrigerated (will keep for about 3 weeks). Makes approx. 500g.

Nectarine or Peach Bread and Butter Pudding

Ingredients:

8-12 Slices of bread and butter,
brioche bread or stale croissant
can be used
3 Nectarines or peaches skinned
and sliced or chopped
A few raspberries or raspberry
puree
4 tbs. Amoretto liquer
3 Eggs
500ml. Single cream
About 10 Amoretti biscuits

Method:

1. Butter an ovenproof dish. Cut
   the slices in half diagonally and
   arrange it over the base of the
   dish.

2. Put fruit in a bowl and pour
   boiling water over it. Leave for a
   minute or two and then remove
   the skin. The skin should slide
   off easily now. Halve the
   nectarines and remove the
   stones.

3. Slice or chop the nectarines and
   spread them over the bread and
   butter, keeping some for the top
   layer. Pour a dribble of raspberry
   puree or a few fresh raspberries
   over the nectarine slices.

4. Crush the Amoretti biscuits and
   layer a couple of handfuls over
   the nectarines and raspberries.

5. Put another layer of bread and
   butter on top and then more fruit
   and puree.

6. Mix together the cream, eggs
   and Amoretto liqueur. Pour the
   mixture over the pudding and
   allow to stand for at least 1/2
   hour. Scatter over the remaining
   amoretti biscuits just before
   cooking.

7. Serve with extra fruit puree.

To Cook

Aga on the grid shelf on the floor
of the roasting oven until just firm to
the touch (should take about
15-25 minutes)

Electric fan oven at 160 °c
(Gas mark 5) for 30 - 40 minutes.
Cook in the combination oven at
180° C with 180 watt microwave
for 15- 20 minutes.

Earl Grey Teabread

I love Earl Grey tea with lemon - this is it in a cake which is even better! This is a really quick recipe and it is ready to eat as soon as it is cold.

Do not panic, I haven't forgotten them - there aren't any eggs in it!

Ingredients:

3 Earl Grey teabags
200ml Boiling water
110 g Butter or margarine
150 g Sultanas or raisins
120 g Soft brown sugar
Zest and rind of a lemon
260 g Self raising flour
1 tsp Baking powder
1 tsp Mixed spice
Pinch of salt

Method:

1. Make the tea and brew for 2 minutes. Pour the tea into a saucepan.

2. Add the butter, sugar, sultanas and the zest and juice of the lemon. Bring to the boil and simmer for 4 minutes. Then let it cool down completely.

3. Baseline a loaf dish or tin.

4. Sieve the dry ingredients into a bowl. Pour in the other ingredients and beat together.

5. Pour into the baking tin or dish to cook. Cook.

   Aga in the baking oven
   for 45 minutes
   Alternatively cook on the grid shelf on the floor of the roasting oven, with the cold shelf going in after 10-15 minutes.
   Total cooking time should be 30-40 minutes.

   Electric fan oven at 150°c (Gas mark 4) for 45 mins
   Cook in the combination oven at 180°C with 180 watt microwave for 18 minutes.

6. Leave in the dish to cool and then let it go cold on a cooling tray.

7. Eat with or without butter and with a cup of Earl Grey to wash it down!

Kiwi Krisps

A recipe picked up in New Zealand. These make a change from Choc chip cookies and are good with or in ice cream!

Ingredients:

100g	Butter
50g	Castor Sugar
150g	Plain Flour
50g	Chocolate Chips, Nuts or Dried Fruit, etc.
1tbs	Condensed Milk
¼ tsp	Vanilla Essence
1tsp	Baking Powder

Method:

1. Cream together the butter, sugar and condensed milk. Add the vanilla essence.

2. Sift in the plain flour and baking powder. Add the chocolate chips.

3. Place teaspoonfuls of the mixture on a lined baking tray and flatten with a fork.

4. Bake:
   Aga in the baking oven for approximately 20 minutes. Alternatively cook on the grid shelf on the floor of the roasting oven for 10 minutes.

   Electric fan oven at 160ºC (Gas mark 5) for 20 minutes.

Ice Cream

There are lots of ice cream cook books. My favourite is Ben and Jerry's which is full of great ideas. For those of you who haven't had the chance to see this book, it contains a couple of basic recipes and, like all my recipes, once you have the basic the options are endless.

Vanilla tends to bring the flavour out when making ice cream. I tend to keep a split vanilla pod in the caster sugar jar too. If you use one in the custard you can wash it, dry it on the Aga and use it again or keep it in the sugar!

A custard base Ingredients:

300ml. Whole milk
2 or 3 Eggs yolks
60 gms. Caster sugar
300ml. Whipping cream
A vanilla pod

Method:

1. Split the vanilla pod and add to the milk as you bring it to the boil. Leave it on one side for 15 minutes to infuse.

2. Beat together the yolks and the sugar. Strain the milk onto the yolks once it has cooled slightly. Heat gently until it starts to coat the back of the spoon, do not let it boil or it could curdle.

   This can be also done at 360 watt in the microwave, stirring every 30 seconds.

3. Leave the custard base to go cold.

4. Whip the cream to soft peaks. Combine the cold custard and the cream and pour into the ice cream maker.

   If you do not have an ice cream maker, put it into the freezer. Allow to half freeze, about an hour. .

   Then take it out and mix it up thoroughly. Replace in the freezer and let it freeze. Always remove from the freezer 1/2 hour before serving.

An ice cream maker is a great investment if you really like ice cream as it churns the mixture until a soft smooth ice cream is formed and ready to be put in a container to store in the freezer,

Many different flavourings can be added to the basic mix. If you are adding a liquid or puree, add it to the custard before folding in to the cream. If you are adding something solid, add it after the ice cream has finished churning and mix it through just before you pack it for the freezer.

Simple Fruit Ice Creams

Ingredients:

400-500 gms. Fruit
100gms. Sugar
500ml. Whipping cream

Method:

1. If the fruit needs cooking, place in a saucepan with 2 tbs of water and cook until soft.

2. Add the sugar, process the fruit and then sieve it. (This means you don't have to top and tail gooseberries and blackcurrants as those bits are left behind in the sieve!)

3. Allow the fruit to become cold. If the fruit doesn't need cooking, i.e. strawberries or raspberries, add a little sugar to taste and puree the fruit.

4. Whip the cream to soft peaks and fold the two mixtures together and put in the ice cream maker or just freeze.

Uncooked Egg Base Ice Cream

This does make a delicious ice cream, but you must be sure of your egg supply. I suggest that you do not serve it to the young, elderly, pregnant or infirm. This is easiest made in an electric mixer.

Ingredients:

2 Eggs
150gms. Caster sugar
450 ml. Double cream
200ml. Milk
1^1/$_2$ tsp. Vanilla essence
OR use vanilla sugar

Method:

1. Beat the eggs until thick and frothy. Gradually add the sugar, beating all the time until really thick and creamy.

2. Mix the cream and milk together (and vanilla essence if using it). Blend in with the egg mixture in the mixer.

3. Pour into the ice cream maker to freeze.

4. If you are adding a puree to this recipe, substitute the puree for the milk.

5. If you are adding solids, fold them into the mixture as you take it out of the ice cream maker to go to the freezer.

Additions

A list compiled with the help of my children (now 23 and 25!):

Crunchie, Maltesers or Caramel chocolate bars can be chopped up and folded in to the frozen ice cream as it goes to the freezer.

Mini marshmallows can be folded in.

For a ripple effect stir fruit puree, chocolate sauce or fudge sauce into the just frozen ice cream i.e. when it is still soft enough to cut through with a spoon.

Dried fruits previously soaked in liquor.

Chopped/whole nuts, praline in big chunks or powdered praline with a little nut liquor (eg Amaretto) can be added to the cream.

Stem ginger or glace ginger with some of the syrup can be added to the cream. Ginger wine can be added, it gives an interesting green tinge to the ice cream!

Uncooked Kiwi Krisps mix or broken up cooked cookies can be stirred in.

Assorted glace fruits, chopped cherries, cut peel, angelica, ginger and a few chopped blanched almonds, with a little kirsch or cointreau.

These are just a few suggestions, let your imagination run riot or let your taste buds dictate! Homemade fruit purees can act as sauces or the fudge or chocolate sauces that are in the book somewhere can be used!

All the sauces just need to be popped on the back of the Aga or in the microwave at 360 watt, so you can serve them warm with your creations!
Fudge Sauce April
Chocolate Sauce September

Sorbet

This is a way of using the egg whites ,left when just making ice cream you will have used yolks for the custard base. It is just a basic sorbet recipe that can be adapted to most fruits.

Ingredients:

400 g Strawberries
100 g Caster sugar or
2 tbs Honey
Juice of a large lemon or ½ glass of champagne
2 Egg whites

Method:

1. Wash, hull and slice the strawberries.

2. Add the sugar or honey, lemon juice or champagne and refrigerate until the sugar has dissolved and the ingredients are well chilled.

3. Mash the ingredients to a puree and pour into the ice cream maker or place in the freezer until softly frozen.

4. Once softly frozen, beat the egg white to a soft snow and fold the two mixtures carefully together. Put in the freezer until needed to eat.

5. This can be frozen without the egg white to just make a water ice.
   Take out of the freezer for 30 minutes before serving.

Best Bitter and a few tablespoonfuls of sugar is another interesting combination!

Elderflower Champagne

When I was first married it was great fun making home made wines from the hedgerows - some were very drinkable, but others were a bit like brass cleaner! I remember the fresh yeast spread on toast floating on the ingredients in a large bowl as the fermentation started. I stopped producing wines when I found my 18 month old daughter having a wonderful time mixing the toast well in by hand, I think some sand had been added too! I have included a very simple refreshing Summer drink, which you might like to try from the hedgerows!

Ingredients;

8 Large heads of Elderflowers
4$\frac{1}{2}$ litres Cold water
700gms. Granulated sugar
Rind and juice of 2 lemons
2 tbs. White wine vinegar

Method:

1. Rinse the Elderflowers and cut the heads off the stalks. Put the in a large container- a stainless steel preserving pan is ideal.

2. Add the rest of the ingredients, cover with a cloth and leave for 4 days - there is natural yeast in the flowers and this will start to ferment.

3. Strain and bottle in strong bottles as they have been known to explode!

4. It can be drunk, well chilled, after 10 days or left to mature into a still wine. But beware - if the wine is kept for over a year it will start to ferment again when it is flowering time the following year, that's nature for you!

July

A lazy month, a hot month hopefully! We don't want to spend too long in the kitchen so most of these recipes can be prepared earlier, ready to serve, or popped in the oven when you are ready to eat.

RECIPES

Ricey Ring

Courgette Pie

Those Sausages

Fish Cakes

Mango Salsa

Kebabs

Ostrich or lamb en croûte

Apricot Marmalade

Gooseberry and Elderflower tart

Hot lemon pudding

Cherry and kirsch bread and butter pudding

Blackcurrant Syllabub

Biscotti

The Three 'C' Cake

Rice Ring

Sorry, I've got 3 ring moulds which I love to use as they always look pretty, so here's another recipe using one! It can of course be done in any dish or even a loose bottomed cake tin.. You can base line it, if you are worried about turning it out! You can take it on a picnic in the tin and turn it out on the serving plate at the picnic. Just a smart fishy rice salad really!

Ingredients:

300 g Long grain or basmati rice
2 tsp. Oil
6 Spring onions
1-2 tsp. Curry paste or powder
300g Cooked smoked fish,
salmon, haddock, cod or trout
4 tbs Mayonnaise
2 Hard-boiled eggs
2 tbs Cooked peas.
2 tbs Chopped parsley
Salt and pepper
1/2 a Cucumber
6 Cherry tomatoes

Method:

1. Cook the rice - this amount is 1³/4cups, so that means 3-3¹/2cups of water (600ml). Rinse the rice to remove excess starch, so that it won't stick. Bring the water to the boil and add the rice to the pan, bring it back to the boil and simmer gently with a well fitting lid on until all the water has been absorbed. This should take 15-30 minutes depending on the rice. With an Aga once it has come to the boil put it in the simmering oven.

2. When the rice is cooked rinse well with cold water and let it cool down slightly.

3. Trim and chop the spring onions and sauté until soft with the oil. Add the curry powder or paste and cook that for a couple of minutes and allow this to cool.

4. Hard boil the eggs.

5. Poach the smoked fish if necessary and cook the peas and let these cool slightly too.

6. Once everything is ready, mix the curry mix with the mayonnaise, chop the hard boiled eggs and combine these with the rice, fish, peas and parsley, adjust the seasoning to taste.

7. Oil a 1¹/2 litre ring mould and while everything is still warm press the mixture firmly into the mould and chill for at least 2 hours.

8. Turn out onto a serving dish, slice enough cucumber to go around the ring and dice the rest. Halve the tomatoes, mix with the diced cucumber and put in the middle of the ring.

9. Serve with green salad and extra mayonnaise on the side, as a starter, lunch or supper.

Courgette Pie

This is a recipe I collected from a very dear friend in New Zealand, who very kindly let me stay for the Millennium, and that was one of the very few times I didn't see New Zealand bathed in sunshine! With all that sun everything grows amazingly well and Nicky always has a glut of courgettes, and this is her family and friends' favourite recipe. It's a great idea too if you are counting the calories, to cook a quiche type filling in the dish without the pastry! A little chopped rosemary and /or garlic and /or mushrooms are good or extra cheese and no courgettes for cheese pie, again endless permutations! It can also be cooked in individual ramekins to serve as a starter, cut the cooking time to 15 minutes approximately.

Ingredients:

500g Courgettes
1 Large onion
300 g Mature cheese
120 g Plain flour
125 ml Vegetable oil
1 tsp Baking powder
5 Eggs
Salt and pepper

To Cook:

Aga on the grid shelf on the floor of the roasting oven for 20-30 minutes until just firm to the touch and golden brown. Or cook on the third set of runners in the baking oven for 40 minutes.

Electric fan oven at 160°c (Gas mark 5) for 40 minutes Serve with a well dressed mixed salad and perhaps some garlic bread!

Method:

1. Wash, trim and chop the courgettes and onions and grate the cheese.

2. Put the eggs in a bowl and beat them lightly and add all the other ingredients and mix well together.

3. Butter a 26 cm ceramic flan dish and pour the mixture in this and cook.

Those Demonstration Sausages!

A quick mention here for those sausages that I cook at demonstrations. Any
old sausages can be improved, if AFTER cooking you toss them in honey
and mustard. If you are a big mustard fan, use equal quantities of runny
honey and whole grain mustard (which I tend to refer to as seedy mustard). If
not so keen, use 1 tsp of mustard to 1tbs of honey. Warm it on the back of
the Aga or give it a quick 30 seconds on maximum in the microwave. Pour
over the cooked sausages and serve on sticks. Stir some mustard and
honey into mayonnaise to serve with them as a dip.

Deluxe Fish Cakes

Another recipe which is easy to adapt to the fish and other ingredients that you like. They can have curry spices added or other herbs and flavourings, eg lemon or lime. Hollandaise sauce could also be served with them or home made tartar sauce. Make the cakes the size that you want, depending on whether they are a starter or a main course.

Ingredients:

200g Smoked cod or haddock
300gms Fresh salmon fillet
100g Fresh cod
Milk and herbs for cooking the fish.
500g Cooked mashed potato
1 Small red onion chopped
2 tbs Capers
2 tbs Chopped parsley or coriander
Whole grain mustard
Optional -1or 2 hard boiled eggs
Salt and pepper
A Dash of Tabasco
Flour for dredging
2 Eggs
Breadcrumbs

Method:

1. Cover the fish with milk and add herbs, lemon rind, peppercorns and a blade of mace if available or just milk!

2. Poach slowly on the hob or in the oven, Aga on the grid shelf on the floor of the roasting oven or at 160ºc (Gas mark 5) for 10 minutes. Remove from the oven and allow to cool in the milk.

3. Sauté the onion in a little butter or oil until soft. Remove the skin and any lurking bones from the fish. Hard boil and chop the eggs if you are including them.

4. To the mashed potato add one fresh egg, about a tsp of mustard, the capers, (chop them if they are very large) the hard boiled egg, herbs, onion seasoning and the fish. Mix well together.

5. On a floured board with floured hands take a spoonful of mixture and shape into "cakes". Place in the refrigerator to firm up.

6. Break an egg in a shallow dish and break up with a fork. Put the breadcrumbs in a polythene bag.

7. Coat the fish cakes first in the egg and the toss them in the breadcrumbs to coat. Reshape if necessary and chill again,

8. They can be fried in shallow fat for about 3 minutes per side, depending on size or they can be cooked on bake-o-glide in the oven.

Aga in the roasting oven on the floor of the oven for 5-10 minutes and then on the top set of runners for 10 more minutes

Electric fan oven at 170°c (Gas mark 6) on the grill rack above the roasting tin for 20 minutes.

Serve with Salsa and stir fried vegetables.

Mango Salsa

Salsas are very popular at the moment and are a good compliment to lots of dishes for a contrast of flavours and textures. You can mix together the ingredients that you enjoy, making it as hot or as mild as you like. It is like getting the ingredients ready for making chutney and forgetting to cook it! Salsas go well with pâtés and cold meats.

Ingredients:

1 Ripe mango, peeled and chopped
1 Red pepper, deseeded and chopped
1 Small red onion, peeled and chopped
$\frac{1}{2}$ Red chilli pepper, deseeded and chopped finely
A good handful of coriander cut up
Juice of $\frac{1}{2}$ a lime
Optional: 1 tbs Capers, chopped

Method:

1. Mix all the ingredients together and chill for at least 2 hours.

2. Check seasoning a little oilive oil can be added, and serve at room temperature with the fish cakes.

Kebabs

Kebabs are easy finger food and could always go out to the barbecue! These are ideas for marinades which can go on most meats cubed and ready to thread.Not only do they add flavour, which becomes more intense the longer it is left, they also help to tenderize the meat . You can use an assortment of vegetables, peppers, mushrooms, onions, whole small tomatoes, apricot halves or even banana chunks. Bear in mind that the vegetables will cook more quickly than the meat so make their size bigger by proportion. All of these could be cooked on a cocktail stick to make a great assortment of instant hot cocktail nibbles, some with dip!

Whenever honey or sugar is included in the marinade, cook with care as they can burn easily, so shake off the excess and only add more at the end of the cooking to enhance the flavour.

You could even do kebabs of garlic bread. Cut the bread into approx. 4 cm cubes or hunks. Melt some butter with garlic and chopped parsley in a large bowl and toss the bread in this. Thread it onto skewers and bake in the oven with the kebabs. They will only take 12 minutes depending on how crispy you want them!

The marinades can also be used for large chicken joints, chops or fish before cooking in the usual way.

Sweet & Sour

A sweet and sour marinade that I like is with apricots - this is excellent with chicken or lamb.

Ingredients:

200ml Wine vinegar
100ml Water
6-8 Fresh apricots well chopped
3 tbs Brown sugar
1 Small onion chopped
1 tbs Curry powder
1 tbs Turmeric
2 Cloves garlic crushed
1 Bay leaf
Salt and pepper

Method:

1. Put all the ingredients in a saucepan and bring to the boil. Simmer for 5 minutes and allow to cool. Pour over the meat and leave overnight at least.

2. Shake off the excess marinade and cook as previously. You can use fresh apricots on the kebabs and a few bay leaves look pretty.

3. Put the remaining marinade in a pan and reheat. Reduce down to a marmalade to go with the kebabs.

500g. Chicken or your choice of meat cut into bite size pieces and then marinaded in one of the marinades listed below:

Teriyaki

(This is also suitable for prawns)

Ingredients:

6 tbs Soy sauce
6 tbs Dry sherry or Rice wine
1 tbs Demerara sugar
1 tbs Grated root ginger
3 Cloves of garlic- crushed
Salt and pepper

Method:

1. Mix all the ingredients together and pour over the meat and marinade over night, or for at least 2 hours.

2. Shake off excess marinade and thread the meat onto the skewers with vegetables if you want. Brush with oil before cooking.

   Serve on a bed of rice with a side salad.

To Cook

Aga on the first or second set of runners in the roasting oven for 15-20 minutes turning at least once.
On the grill rack in the roasting tin.

Electric fan oven at 180°c (Gas mark 7) for 15-20 minutes. Alternatively cook under a radiant grill, turning frequently, brushing with more marinade if necessary.

Hob

Cook in a well pre-heated ridged grill pan on the hob, turning frequently so the kebab has all around stripes. Always oil the meat and not the pan (you can pre-heat the pan in the roasting oven with an Aga and finish off the cooking in there too!)

Satay & Peanut sauce

Ingredients:

1 Medium red onion chopped
2 Cloves garlic crushed
1 tsp Ground cumin
2 tsp Ground coriander
A few drops of Tabasco sauce
Zest and juice of a lemon
1/2 tbs Brown sugar
4 tbs Creamy coconut milk
4 tbs Olive oil

For the sauce:

200gms Crunchy peanut butter
Salt and pepper

Method:

1. Mix all the main ingredients together and marinade the meat for a minimum of 2 hours. You can add the vegetables for the last 15 minutes if you want to.

2. Thread the meat and vegetables on skewers and cook as before. Save 4 tbs of the marinade to brush over the kebabs in the last few minutes of cooking.

3. Heat the rest of the marinade in a pan with the peanut butter. Season to taste. If the sauce is too thick add more creamy coconut.

4. Serve as a sauce with the kebabs on rice, or as a dip with nibbles on cocktail sticks.

Yogurt Marinade

Make up two lots of this separately -
one for the marinade and one
for the sauce

Ingredients:

To a small pot of natural yogurt add:
The zest and juice of a
lemon or lime
1-2 tbs Chopped mint or coriander
A good dash of Tabasco OR
1/4 tsp. Cayenne pepper
A Cushed clove of garlic
Salt to taste

Method:

1. Mix all the ingredients together and continue as above.

2. For the sauce you can add about 12 cm cucumber diced to the sauce. Mix and season well and serve with the kebabs separately.

Apricote Marmalade

Ingredients:

500g Apricots, stoned and chopped or 300g of dried apricots soaked overnigh
200 g Onions, chopped
4 tbs Wine vinegar
100g Soft brown sugar
A sprig of rosemary

Method:

1. Put all the ingredients in a saucepan with the lid on and cook:

2. **Aga** on the floor of the roasting oven for 15 minutes. Take from the oven stir well and return to the oven with the lid off. Cook until reduced and soft - it should be a slightly caramely marmalade, about 15-25 minutes Allow to cool before serving warm as it can burn if served too hot.

On the hob

Simmer on the hob at a low setting for 15 minutes with the lid on and then remove the lid and increase the heat and cook until reduced and soft, stirring often.

3. Serve with the Lamb, it will keep in a screw top jar in the refrigerator, but is best served at room temperature.

Lamb en Croûte (or Ostrich!)

Ostrich is an interesting alternative. I demonstrated this is South Africa, where they have a lot of ostrich! It is similar in texture to fillet steak and like steak should not be overcooked. Ostrich has a milder flavour and benefits from having flavours added, hence this farce is ideal! Graham Douglas, my friendly Newport Pagnall butcher, manages to get Ostrich for me, it is a very tender meat and is very good for those on a low cholesterol diet.

Lamb en Croûte Ingredients:

A 7 or 8 rib length of loin of lamb in one piece, boned.
or a 600g piece of ostrich meat
30 g Butter
2 tbs Oil
Seasoning

For the farce:

3 Cloves of garlic
1 tbs Chopped mint
A sprig of rosemary chopped
150 g Chopped dried, ready to eat apricots
150 g Onion
5 Slices of fresh bread made into breadcrumbs
Salt and pepper
A packet of ready-made puff pastry
1 Egg for egg wash

Method:

1. Melt the butter and oil in the roasting tin. Take the skin and any excess fat off the lamb. Season the boned loin joint and skewer or tie it together and seal it in the roasting tin on the floor of the roasting oven or the Aga, 10 minutes each side OR in an electric fan oven 180ºc (Gas mark 7) for 20-30 minutes.

2. Allow to cool and then remove from the pan.

3. Put all the farce ingredients in a processor and whiz until they start to bind together.

4. Roll out the pastry to a large oblong. Put half of the farce on the centre section and put the now cold meat on top and the rest of the farce on this. Cut a small square of pastry out of each corner, and fold the pastry neatly around the meat using egg wash as glue to seal the parcel.(Nice hospital corners!)

5. Turn it over and place on a bake-o-glide lined baking tray. Decorate with the scraps of pastry, cut into lamb shapes or ostrich! Or just leaves and brush with egg wash to glaze.

Aga on the floor of the roasting oven for approximately 45 minutes until golden brown.

Electric fan oven at 170°c (Gas mark 6) for 45 minutes
Serve with Apricot Marmalade, posh mash and carrots.

Gooseberry and Elderflower Tart

Sweet Pastry Ingredients:

340g Plain flour
250 g Butter
1 tbs Sugar
1 Egg yolk (make up to 50 ml with water, usually 2 tbs.)

Gooseberry and Mint curd Ingredients:

500 g Gooseberries with
2 tbs Water
200g Sugar
150 g Butter
3 Eggs well beaten
3 Large heads of Elderflowers

Method:

1. Place the flour, butter and sugar in the processor and mix to fine breadcrumbs.

2. Add the egg and water mixture and mix in until it starts to bind together. Remove and knead gently to a ball.

3. Cover the pastry with cling or put in a polythene bag and refrigerate for approximately 30 minutes until firm.

4. Roll out the pastry onto a floured board to line a fluted flan dish or tin. See rolling tips in January.

5. Prick the base of flan and refrigerate to chill pastry before cooking. (If you are using a ceramic dish, remember to remove the dish from the refridgerator prior to cooking to allow dish to adjust to room temperature before placing into the hot oven)

Method:

1. Place gooseberries, water and Elderflowers in a saucepan and bring to the boil and simmer on a very low heat until very tender. In the Aga move the saucepan into the simmering oven until the berries are tender (approx. 1 hour)

2. Put this mixture through a sieve to form puree.

3. Place butter, sugar and fruit puree into a large bowl and melt together. If you have an Aga do this in a bowl over a pan of simmering water on the simmering plate. Alternatively in a microwave oven at 650 watt for 3 minutes.

4. Stir well and strain in the beaten eggs. Continue to cook. If using an Aga, stir over the pan of simmering water until the curd thickens.

In the microwave, cook at 360 watt
for 1 minute. Stir and then cook for
30 seconds at a time at 360 watt
until a creamy curd is made.
Pot and cover. Keep refrigerated
(will keep for about 3 weeks).

The Tart Ingredients:

350 ml. Cream (single or double)
3/4 Pot of gooseberry and
Elderflower curd
2 or 3 Eggs (depending on size of
flan dish)

Method:

1. Mix the above ingredients
   together and pour into the
   prepared pastry case and cook.

2. **Aga** on the floor of the oven for
   20-30 minutes until the pastry is
   brown and the filling is just firm.

   Electric Cook in the fan oven at
   180°c (Gas mark 7)
   for 35-40 minutes
   If you have an oven with bottom
   heat cook on this function, in the
   roasting tin, on the lowest shelf
   position, at 200°c for 30-40
   minutes

3. Allow to cool completely and
   serve cold dusted with icing
   sugar and elderflowers
   at the side.

Hot Lemon Pudding

I do like my steamed puds, even in the summer. This is one I don't do often, but I think I should! It tastes like lemon meringue pie, but is less trouble and rather pretty!

Ingredients:

100g Butter
100 g Caster sugar
2 Egg yolks
100 g Fresh breadcrumbs
Zest and juice of 1 lemon
1/2 tsp. baking powder
To serve:
2 Egg whites
75 g Caster sugar
1 Eating apple with red skin

Method:

1. Cream together the butter and sugar and beat in the egg yolks.

2. Add the zest, juice and breadcrumbs, and finally the baking powder.

3. Place in a base lined soufflé dish or pudding basin and cover with foil or a lid.

4. **Aga:** Steam in a saucepan with 10cms water in the bottom on the floor of the roasting oven for 15 minutes and then transfer to the simmering oven for a further hour.

   Electric or gas bring to the boil on the hob and then reduce the heat and simmer very gently for 11/2hours, check that the water level keeps topped up.

5. Beat the egg whites until stiff. Add a 1/3rd and beat well, add another 1/3rd and beat again. Then fold in the rest of the sugar with the cored and diced apple. I leave the peel on if it is a red apple as I like the colour and the texture.

6. Spread this as a wide band on the edge of a serving plate and quickly brown.
   Aga roasting oven for 3-5 minutes or
   Electric fan oven at 200°C (Gas Mark 8) for 3-5 minutes.

7. When the lemon pudding is cooked turn it out into the centre of the plate and the meringue is the sauce!

Cherry and Kirish Bread and Butter Pudding

Ingredients:

250 g Fresh cherries stoned
4-6 tbs Kirsch
A Loaf of brioche
Butter
30ml. Single cream
2 Large Eggs
2 tbs Demerara sugar

Method:

1   Cut the brioche into $1^1/2$ cm thick slices and butter. Butter an ovenproof dish and line it with bread.

2. Stone the cherries - a cherry stoner is a useful investment, always handy at this time of the year! Put $3/4$ of these in the dish, arrange the remaining brioche and butter in the dish and top with the remaining cherries.

3. Beat together the cream, eggs and the kirsch and pour into the dish. Allow to stand for at least 30 minutes and sprinkle the demerara over the pudding and bake.

    Aga on the grid shelf on the floor of the roasting oven for 15-20 minutes until just set.

    Electric fan oven at 170°c (Gas mark 6) for 20-30 minutes. Combination oven cook 180°c with 180 watt microwave for 15 minutes.

Blackcurrent Syllabub

Ingredients:

400g Blackcurrants
100 g Sugar
100 ml Rose wine
70 g Caster sugar
Juice of a small lemon
250ml. Double cream
A few toasted flaked almonds

Method:

1. Prepare the blackcurrants and rinse in a colander. Put in a saucepan and add 2tbs. water, heat gently and simmer very gently for 20 minutes add the sugar and allow to cool.

2. Put the wine, caster sugar and lemon juice in a bowl and chill overnight. Stir well and then add the cream and whip until light and fluffy.

3. Put 2 tbs of the blackcurrants in a wine glass and top with syllabub. Finish with a sprinkling of flaked almonds.

4. Serve with biscotti!

Biscotti

Ingredients:

250 g Plain flour
1/2 tsp. Baking powder
150 g Caster sugar
65 g Butter
2 Eggs
1/2 tsp. Almond essence
50 g Pistachio nuts
100 g Whole hazelnuts
A little extra caster sugar

Method:

1. Put the flour, caster sugar, baking powder and the butter, cut up, in the food processor and process to the breadcrumb stage. Add the almond essence and the eggs and process until it binds together. Turn out onto a floured board and knead in the whole nuts.

2. Line a baking tray with bake-o-glide. Shape the dough into a sausage about 30-35 cm long, put on the baking tray and flatten slightly and bake.

3. **Aga** in the baking oven for 30 minutes on the third set of runners.
   Alternatively cook in the roasting oven on the bottom set of runners. Put the cold shelf above after 10 minutes and cook 10 more minutes.

   Electric fan oven at 160°c (Gas mark 5) for 30 minutes until golden

4. Remove from the oven and leave to cool for 20 minutes. Cut up into 1-2 cm thick slices, replace on the baking tray and return to the oven.

5. **Aga** cook in the simmering oven for 30 minutes
   Electric fan oven at 150°c (Gas mark 3) for 30 minutes until it is dried out.

The biscotti are a good contrast to syllabub, but are also excellent for coffee dunking!

Coke Crater Cake (The 3 "C" Cake)

This sneaked in for the 4th July! The first time I cooked this cake for a demonstration was on an American tour, but it has become a great favourite everywhere. It is Anglicized with melted butter instead of groundnut oil, but is a very easy fun cake and the gooiest most divine pud whilst it is still warm with home made vanilla ice cream!!

Ingredients:

250 g Butter, melted
250 g Self raising
1 tsp. Bicarbonate of soda
100 gms Soft brown sugar
100 g Caster sugar
60 g Cocoa powder
150 ml. Coke
2 Large eggs
1 tsp. Vanilla essence
100g White mini marshmallows

For the Topping:

150g Plain chocolate
4 tbs Coke
100g White mini marshmallows

Method:

1. Put the butter in a jug and allow to melt on the back of the Aga, or in the microwave for 2 minutes at 600 watt covered with kitchen paper, to stop it splashing and making a mess.

2. Place the flour, sugars, cocoa powder and bicarbonate of soda in a bowl and mix together.

3. Add the eggs, coke, vanilla essence and melted butter to the bowl and beat well together. Then fold in the marshmallows and put in a buttered spring clip tin and bake. Alternatively cook in the 20 cm tin lined with bake-o-glide in the cake baker.

4. **Aga** in the baking oven for 1 hour OR in the cake baker for an hour.

   Electric fan oven at 160°c (Gas Mark 5) for an hour.

5. Melt the chocolate with the coke on the back of the Aga or in the microwave at 360 watt for 4 minutes, or over hot water. Stir this well together and pour over the cake while it is still warm. Then put all the marshmallows on top and allow to set. Remove from the tin. The cake is also delicious warm with ice cream as a pud!

To remove the cake from the cake baker tin: allow the topping to set completely and run a palette knife between the bake-o-glide and the tin. Cover the whole thing with cling film and turn the cake out onto this (the marshmallows act as a cushion!) Then quickly turn the cake the right way up onto a plate, removing the bake-o-glide as you do so!

August

Summer holidays, long days to fill, and children to occupy and feed! Alfresco meals, lazy days and children's tea parties! So here are some ideas of my favourites for the family (i.e. the children!) to cook.
Summer flavours and aromas to bottle to brighten the Winter in oils and vinegars.

RECIPES

Filo Prawn Parcels

Cold Curry Chicken

Easy blender home made Mayonnaise

Tom's Chicken

Susie's Pizza

Salmon Plait

Cheese Surprise Meatballs

The Glorius 12th

Wine Stock

Cauliflower Cheese Meal

Meringues

Meringue Gateau

Buttercream

Meringue and Walnut, Chocolate Pyramid

Toblerone Dip

Speedy Bread and Butter Pudding

Chocolate Krispies

Lemon Drizzle Cake

Kiddy Kakes

Boiled Fruit Cake

Herby Vinegars

Chilli and, or Garlic oils

Raspberry Vinegar

Filo Prawn Parcels

This is the recipe for an easy starter that my son Tom has been using forever. The recipe uses filo pastry, but you could use ready made puff pastry.

Ingredients:

1pkt Fresh Filo Pastry
200 g Peeled Prawns
100gGarlic & Herb Cheese Cream
80 g Butter
Sesame Seeds or Poppy seeds

Method:

1. Melt the butter on the back of the Aga or in the microwave at 360 watt for 1-2 minutes

2. Cut the Filo Pastry into 20 cm squares.

3. Place a few prawns in the middle of an edge of the pastry and put a small knob of cheese on the prawns. Fold in the sides and roll up the pastry around the prawns and place on a lined baking tray.

4. Brush over with butter and sprinkle with seeds and cook:

Aga in the baking oven for 10-15 minutes until golden brown.

Electric fan oven at 180°c (Gas mark 6) for 15 minutes

5. Serve on a bed of fresh salad leaves with mayonnaise. If you like ginger, you can add some grated root ginger to the mayonnaise or you can add whatever you do like!
(Ketchup is good, with garlic - that way not everyone recognizes that famous brand!)

Alternative fillings:

Cooked spinach added to sautèed onion and garlic, well seasoned with cumin.

Mashed Stilton cheese with chopped walnuts and chopped parsley.

Grated carrot, cream cheese, orange zest and raisins.

Finely chopped cooked ham with cream cheese and fresh red currants or dried cranberries and herbs.
Mashed tined tuna, with turmeric, caper, lemon zest and cream cheese.

Garlic and herb cheese with chopped sun dried tomatoes (the ones in oil) and basil.

These are just a few thoughts, which I'm sure you can improve upon. You can, of course, put three squares of pastry brushed with butter at right angles on top of each other and then put the filling in the middle and lift up the corners and form a purse for a change.

Cold Curried Chicken

This is a classic that I have done a different way and with different ingredients each time! I have never written down what I put in it before so this is an ideal time to work it out! The Perfect Picnic Party Piece, son et lumieres, sports days, speech days all the Summer season! (should have been in June so that it could do the whole season. try it next Ascot, Wimbolden and Henley!)

Ingredients:

1¹/2 kg Cooked chicken (or 6 cooked chicken breasts, poached gives the best result).
2 tbs Oil
1 Small onion
1 Red pepper
2 tsp Curry powder or paste
2 tsp Tomato paste
4 tbs White wine
2 tbs Mango chutney
400 ml Mayonnaise
3 tbs Double cream
2 tbs Desiccated coconut or Ground almonds
Zest and juice of ¹/2 lemon
A few toasted flaked almonds
Fresh coriander

Method:

1. To cook the chicken: Place it in a pan with a little water and wine, a carrot, an onion, a few herbs and salt & pepper. Cook covered for 40 minutes or the bird is just tender. The chicken breasts will only need 15-20 minutes. Allow to go cold in the liquid.

2. Prepare and chop the onion and red pepper. Put the oil in a pan and sauté the onion and pepper. Add the curry powder and cook for 2 minutes. Add the tomato puree and the wine and reduce by half. Take from the heat and allow to cool.

3. Take the meat off the chicken, discarding the skin, and cut into large bite size pieces.

4. When it is cold sieve the curry mix into the mayonnaise and add the mango chutney and coconut or almonds. Add the lemon zest and lemon juice if necessary, whip the cream and fold this in. Check the seasoning to taste.

5. Coat the chicken with the mayonnaise sauce and sprinkle over some flaked almonds. Cut up the coriander over it.

6. Serve with the Ricey ring from July (omitting the fish!) or with new potatoes and mixed salad. You can add grapes and olives to the salad if you want.

Transports easily in a tub or box and then just pile onto a plate in a nest of lettuce leaves to serve at your picnic, with cold new potatoes or the rice ring and a green salad.

Easy Blender Mayonnaise

This is a handy recipe - I'm always running out of mayonnaise in the holidays.

Ingredients:

1 Large egg or 2 egg yolks
1 tsp Made mustard
1/2 tsp Caster sugar
1 tbs White wine vinegar
Salt and pepper
200ml. Lght oil, sunflower,
Groundnut or olive or a
combination
A squeeze of lemon juice

Method:

1   Put the egg, mustard, sugar, vinegar, salt and pepper into the processor and whiz until well blended.

2. With the motor running, very slowly add the oil. You will hear a change in sound as it starts to emulsify and thicken. When you have added all the oil, take the mayonnaise out of the processor and add a little lemon juice if you like to your taste. If the mayonnaise is too thick gently add a little boiling water.

3. Store in a jar in the refrigerator.

Tom's Chicken

When he was really very young Tom used to make his version with the left over roast chicken. He got a great sense of satisfaction from making his own tea!

Ingredients:

100 g cooked chicken or ham
16 cm Cucumber
Salad cream
A few lettuce leaves

Method:

1. Cut the cucumber into two 8 cm pieces and cut out the middle leaving a tube.

2. Chop up the middle of the cucumber and the chicken into small pieces.
   Fold in enough salad cream to coat them.

3. Pile this mixture into the cucumber towers. The extra can go in small lettuce leaves served around the towers, instant tea!

This can be done using tomato halves or courgettes as boats! Sarah's version of this used chopped tomato, crabsticks and salad cream. Sarah used to (and still does!) love those synthetic fish sticks. The first time she was given real crab as a treat, however, she refused to eat it because it didn't taste like her beloved crabsticks!

Author's note: I want to be in the book too!!!!!!

My daughter Sarah has very kindly been proof reading and doing the spelling and puctuation, as apparently I don't know what full stops are?? !She felt that Tom was getting more mentions so she added her own little bit here!

Susie's Pizza

This is recipe that I gleaned from a best friend from college days. It is so quick and easy that the kids can make their own pizza. The recipe has no yeast in it but there's still a great sense of achievement for them to make the whole pizza from start to finish!

Ingredients:

340g Self raising flour
170 ml Warm water
130 ml Vegetable oil
80g Grated cheese
1/2 tsp Made English mustard
(or mustard powder)
Salt and pepper

Topping:

1 tin Chopped tomatoes
1 Small onion chopped
2 tbs Grated cheese plus sliced or cubed cheese to top off

Extras:

Assorted vegetables cut up small and tossed in oil, cut up bacon, cooked sausages, herbs, olives, tined fish, fresh cooked prawns or ham or chicken - the list is endless!

Method:

1. Mix together the flour, oil, water, grated cheese and mustard to form a dough and roll out to line a 30 cm tin.

2. Mix together the tinned tomatoes, onion and 2 tbs grated cheese and spread this over the base. Then top with whatever you like and then more cheese if you want to. Bake.

Aga on the floor of the roasting oven for 15 minutes and then move to the bottom set of runners for 10-15 mins and the top is bubbly brown.

Electric fan oven at 180°c (Gas mark 7) for 15-25 minutes

Salmon Plait

Another movable feast. You can have it with salad and mayonnaise or hot with hollandaise and fresh green vegetables and new potatoes.
Pastry foods are always good for picnics as they are ready wrapped!

Ingredients:

1 Packet Puff Pastry
40g Butter
1 Small Onion, chopped
350g Cooked Salmon ,(can be a tin of)
4tbs Sour Cream (or Ordinary Cream with Lemon Juice)
2 tbs Chopped Parsley
Salt and pepper
1 Egg for egg wash

Method:

1. Sauté the onion in the butter.

2. Break up the salmon in a bowl, removing all the bones. Then add all the other ingredients and mix together.

3. Roll out the puff pastry to a large oblong (refer to the Sausage plait recipe in March, to see the pictures of how to do this.) Visualizing the pastry in three sections, cut in from either side towards the centre section with slightly diagonal cuts about 2cm apart.

4. Place the filling down the centre and, picking up alternate strips plait the pastry over the salmon.

5. Brush with egg wash and cook.

   Aga on the floor of the roasting oven for about 1/2 hour.

   Electric fan oven at 170°c (Gas mark 6) for 30 minutes Combination oven 200°c 180 watt microwave for 20 minutes

Cheese Surprise Meetballs

These are tasty and fun to do, wet hands stop the meat sticking to your hands!

Ingredients:

30g Butter or 1 tbs oil
300g Minced Beef i.e. Ground Beef
1 Egg
1 Medium Onion
60 g Fresh Breadcrumbs
100g Cubed Firm Cheese -
such as Cheddar
Oil or butter to fry meatballs

Sauce:

A tin of Tomatoes
80 g Grated Cheese
Herbs of your choice - marjoram or
chopped basil are good

Method:

1. Melt the butter in a large pan and fry the onions until just soft.

2. Add the onions to the mince, along with the breadcrumbs, egg and seasoning and mix well together.

3. Cut the cheese into 2 cm cubes and wrap some mince around each cube of cheese, do this with wet hands, toss the balls in a bowl with flour in.

4. Melt more butter and oil in the pan and brown the meatballs on all sides.

5. Pour the sauce ingredients over the meatballs. At this point add your favourite herbs. Bring this to the boil and cook. The cooking times given are for just one layer of meatballs. If the meatballs are heaped up, leave them in the oven for a little longer. Try to have a single layer if possible.

6. **Aga** cooking in the simmering oven for 45 minutes-1 hour.

   Electric simmer very gently on the hob for 30-45 minutes.

   Serve with Posh Mash with cheese, herbs and mustard mashed in and a green vegetable or salad.

The Glorious 12th Grouse!!

Not really one for the children, but a childhood memory for me. My family and I were always on holiday in Southport at The Clifton in August. The menu there on the 12th always had white heather on, and there was Grouse on the menu. I'm not quite sure how they managed to have it ready for that evening, but I enjoyed the tender bird with a rich gravy.

Grouse To cook

The bird is best hung for a week or more, depending on your taste. Young birds should be quickly roasted for 25-30 minutes
Butter the bird inside and out. Squeeze the juice of a lemon over it and cover well with bacon to keep the meat moist. Remove the bacon for the last 10 minutes to allow the bird to brown.
Serve with a rich gravy made in the roasting tin with the sediment and using some wine stock. You can also add some dried or frozen cranberries and some diced apple to the gravy. Serve with bread sauce, game chips, fresh vegetables and lots of watercress strewn about - Glorious!

Wine Stock

Making your own stock is so satisfying and this is an excellent rich stock.

Ingredients:

500 g Bones from the butcher plus the fat and trimmings, or game carcasses
4 Onions chopped
2 Carrots chopped
Bay leaf, parsley, thyme and sage or a bouquet garni
2 tbs. Wine vinegar
2 tsp. Sugar
3 Tomatoes, quartered
A bottle of red wine
250 ml. Water
Salt and pepper

Method:

1. Place the bones, fat and trimming in a roasting tin or a large saucepan and put it on the floor of the roasting oven or in elecgtric fan oven at 180ºC (Gas Mark 7) for 20 minutes. Add the onions and carrots and mix in with the bones. Let them soften for about 10 more minutes in the oven. Then add the wine vinegar.

2. Move all the ingredients to the stock pot, bring to the boil and add the remaining ingredients, simmer for 1 1/2 hours.
Aga put this in the simmering oven for at least 2 1/2 hours, or on the hob with very gentle heat.

3. Strain the stock and return to the pan. Bring to the boil and reduce. In an Aga this can be done on the floor of the roasting oven for 20-30 minutes.

4. Let it go cold and store in the refrigerator until needed or freeze, in small cartons.

Cauliflower Cheese

An old favourite that can be elevated from a vegetable to a meal in itself. As a matter of habit, I add a little mustard when making a cheese sauce.
I'm not sure whether this is an old wives tale, but I think it helps one to digest the cheese! I use the vegetable water to make the sauce, as most vitamins in vegetables are water soluble, so use the water to make the sauce
and save those vitamins!

Ingredients:

1 Large cauliflower
About 10 small new potatoes
6-8 Cherry tomatoes
1 Onion
70 g Butter
60 g Plain flour
350gms Strong mature Cheddar
1 tsp. Dry mustard powder
1/4 tsp. Cayenne pepper
Salt
Optional: 2 tbs. Breadcrumbs and
1 tbs. Chopped fresh herbs

Method:

1. Peel and chop the onion. Boil well covered with water for 5-10 minutes.

2. Break the cauliflower up into florets and scrub the potatoes. Bring some water to the boil and add both the cauliflower and the potatoes. Cook for just 5 minutes and drain immediately, keeping the water.

3. Drain the onion and keep that water too.

4. Melt the butter in a saucepan and stir in the flour. Slowly add firstly the onion water and then enough cauliflower water to give a smooth coating sauce. Add the onions to this. Also add most of the cheese along with the mustard and the cayenne. Season to taste.

5. In a buttered ovenproof dish
   arrange the cauli, potatoes and
   whole cherry tomatoes and pour
   the sauce evenly over these.
   Sprinkle over the remaining
   cheese. This can be mixed with
   the breadcrumbs and herbs to
   give a crispier finish. Cook.

Aga in the top half of the roasting
oven for 20-30 minutes until
golden brown.

Electric fan oven at 170°c
(Gas mark 6) for 20-30 minutes
Combination fan oven180°c
with 360 watt microwave
for 10-15 minutes

Meringues

A standby for any time - the mixture can be piped, spooned or heaped, large or small to suit most occasions.   The perfect Summer pudding must be raspberries, meringue and cream!

The basic recipe can be added to with nuts, chocolate, coffee, dried fruit or you can just substitute half of the castor sugar for soft brown sugar to give a lovely caramelly flavour, the basic proportions stay the same. You can add 1/2 a teaspoon of food colouring if you need certain colours for a special occasion. Assorted pastel meringues look really pretty just piled in a sparkling crystal bowl.

After making meringues there are always the egg yolks to deal with, and you can deal extremely well with them by adding them to pastry or making a buttercream, which keeps and freezes for future use, so this recipe follows on.

Meringue Gateau Ingredients:

4 Egg whites
110 g Caster sugar

Method:

1. Put the eggs into a cold bowl and whisk until really stiff. Divide the sugar into three portions and add one third and whisk again until stiff. Add the next third and whisk again and then fold in the final third. This will give a firm glossy meringue which you can pipe or spoon onto a bake-o-glide lined baking sheet.

2. For a meringue gateau, put the meringue in a piping bag with a plain vegetable pipe and pipe three 20cm circles. One can be sprinkled with flaked almonds-this will be the top one! If you have spare meringue, pipe small dots and these can be used to decorate the top layer, if they aren't eaten first!

3. Bake. Meringues are cooked when they come off the bake-o-glide easily. This is a matter of personal taste too - I like meringues crisp, but if you prefer a softer centre remove them from the oven earlier. If they are dry and crisp they will keep in an airtight tin for a long time.

4. You can then sandwich the layers together with fruit and cream with a couple of tablespoons of liqueur for good measure!

   Alternatively fold 2 tbs of praline into some cream OR melt 100g of chocolate and fold this into some whipped double cream. Then spread over one layer and put fruit, fresh or pureed, mixed with cream in the other layer and top with the almond layer and dust with icing sugar

To Bake:

Aga in the simmering oven in the middle of the oven for 3-5 hours

Electric fan oven at 50°c (Gas mark 1/4) for 4 hrs.

Butter Cream

Ingredients:

160g Granulated or Caster Sugar
4 Egg Yolks
150ml Water
250g Unsalted Butter softened

Method:

1. Heat the sugar and water to the thin thread stage - a sugar thermometer makes this very easy - it needs to be at 100ºc. To test: Wet your fingers with very cold water and then very quickly dip a finger in the syrup and pinch between the thumb and finger and it should break like glass. Remove from the heat and dip the base of the pan in water to stop it over cooking.

2. Beat the yolks well in an electric mixer and pour the syrup in a steady stream onto the beaten egg yolks, beating all the time until really thick and mousse-like.

3. Cream the softened butter and add, very gradually, to the egg and sugar mixture.

4. Flavour to your taste with grated rind of citrus fruits, melted chocolate, raspberry puree or coffee essence, chopped nuts, ground nuts - the choice is endless.

5. This freezes well and keeps for at least a fortnight in the refrigerator.

Meringue and Walnut Chocolate Pyramid

Here's a good recipe idea: make up the meringue and shape into spoonfuls or pipe into 5-6 cm rosettes. Once cooked and cold, sandwich the meringues together into a pyramid with buttercream with chopped walnuts added to it and pour over chocolate sauce just before serving.
This has the advantage that it can be made up well in advance and comes to no harm. If you use cream the meringues immediately start to soften, but I actually like them like that!

This has to be here as it can be made so easily and lots of sauce is used through the Summer holidays - especially on ice cream!

Chocolate Sauce Ingredients:

100 g Plain chocolate
40 g Butter
3 tbs Water (this can be alcohol instead, not for the children you understand!)

Method:

1. Melt all the ingredients together on the back of the Aga or in the microwave at 360 watt for 3 minutes.

2. With a whisk, whisk until smooth -pour over meringues, ice cream or pudding. Enjoy!

Toblerone Dip

My daughter and son insisted that I include this in August, as it is the perfect garden pud for them!

Ingredients:

1 Large block of Toblerone
300ml Cream any type

To serve an assortment of:

Strawberries
Cherries
Bite size pieces of:
Peaches
Nectarines
Bananas
Apples
And lots of marshmallows
Forks!

Method:

1. Break up the chocolate into pieces in a wide bowl and add the cream.

2. Melt on the back of the Aga or in the microwave at 360 watt for 4-5 minutes.

3. Stir until the chocolate and cream have blended together and serve.

Place on an old garden table and hand out forks and say go. This is not one to be eaten inside, as it can get messy!

Speedy Bread and Butter Pudding

A different presentation this month, just fold in small pieces of fresh fruit, frozen fruit or Dolly Mixtures!

Ingredients:

6 Thick slices of bread
3 Large tbs of dried fruit or what you will!
60 g Butter
200ml. Milk
1 tbs Caster sugar
2 Large eggs
1-2 tbs Demerara sugar

To Cook:

Aga on the grid shelf on the floor of the roasting oven for 15-20 minutes

Electric fan oven at 170°c (Gas mark 6) for 20 minutes. Combination oven 180°C with 360 watt microwave for 10-12 minutes.

Method:

1. Remove the crusts from the bread and cut into cubes and place in a mixing bowl and mix in your chosen fruit or sweeties.

2. Butter an ovenproof dish. Separate the eggs.

3. Put the remaining butter and the milk in a saucepan and melt the butter, do not let it boil. Remove from the heat and pour over the egg yolks and castor sugar and stir together, pour this over the cubed bread mix.

4. Whisk the egg whites to a firm snow and fold in the bread mix and tip into the buttered dish and sprinkle over the demerara sugar and cook.

   For a change melt 2 tbs jam with 2 tbs water to make a jam sauce to go with the pudding.

Chocolate Krispies

My Mother made thousands of these in my, and my children's, childhood. For her it had to be Dairy Milk Chocolate, melting on the Rayburn! Ann, a second cousin delighted in telling her mother as she collected her from a party that she had eaten 20 and she had the cases to prove it! No syrup or sugar just chocolate and krispies, but plenty of chocolate (Sarah prefers Galaxy!) that you, sorry, I mean your children, will enjoy!

Ingredients:

150 g Milk chocolate
80 g Rice Krispies
Paper cake cases

Method:

1. Melt the chocolate in a big bowl on the back of the Aga, or in the microwave at 360 watt for 3-4 minutes.
2. Stir in the krispies until well coated with chocolate, and put spoonfuls of this into paper cases and allow to set in a cold place.

Drizzle Cake

This is one of Tom's favourites. I'm in trouble because I haven't made it for ages!

Ingredients:

The Cake:
100g Margarine
150g Caster sugar
150g Self Raising flour
2 Large eggs
Zest of a large lemon
Pinch of salt

The Topping:

The juice of a large lemon
80 g Icing sugar or castor sugar

Method:

1. Put all the ingredients in a bowl and beat thoroughly together. If the mixture is stiff add a little warm water or milk. Place in a well greased loose bottomed tin or a lined 20 cm tin and bake.

2. **Aga** in the baking oven for 50 minutes to 1 hour or in a cake baker on the floor of the roasting oven for about an hour.

   Electric fan oven at 160°C (Gas mark 4) for about an hour

3. Take from the oven, but leave in the tin.

4. Dissolve the sugar in the lemon juice. Prick the top surface of the cake with a skewer and drizzle over all the hot lemon syrup.

5. Allow to go cold in the tin.

Kiddy Kakes

First make the drizzle cake mixture up. The lemon zest can be left out and 1tsp of vanilla essence can be added instead. Alternatively you could take out a large tablespoon of flour from the ingredients and add that amount of drinking chocolate instead.

The mixture can then be cooked in paper cases in a bun tin. This makes little cakes which can be decorated with icing and smartie faces or can make into butterfly cakes or top hats, holiday fun!

Aga on the grid shelf on the floor of the roasting oven for 10-15 minutes

Electric fan oven 170ºc (Gas mark 6) for 15 minutes approximately

To Decorate Ingredients:

Icing sugar
Margarine or Butter
Smarties, jelly tots, chocolate buttons, dolly mixtures-Whatever is in the sweetie drawer!
Food colouring
Jam

Plan of Attack:

1. You can use either water icing or butter icing for the cakes:

2. To make water icing: sieve icing sugar in a bowl. Add water (or lemon juice) a tablespoon at a time to give a thickish icing that will gently spread when put on the cakes. This can be coloured if required!

3. To make a butter icing: beat up 60g of margarine or butter and mix in 100gof icing sugar. Add 2-3 tsp drinking chocolate powder if you want chocolate icing. This can also be coloured if you want.

Butterfly Cakes and Top Hat Cakes

To make butterfly cakes or top hat cakes: With a 2-3 cm cutter, cut out the centre to about half the depth of the cake. If you give the cutter a wiggle it will come out! Put a small dot of jam in the hole and then a small teaspoonful of butter cream.

Place the piece of sponge back on top to form a top hat.

Alternatively cut the sponge into two pieces and place these on the buttercream to form wings. Dust with icing sugar.

Faces

Make white or pink water icing. Put a teaspoonful of icing on each cake and decorate with smarties etc. Some yellow icing can be made to trickle around the edges for hair! Or just make wonderful colours of icing and do "pretty" patterns!

Mice, ladybirds or hedgehogs.

Take the cake out of its paper case and turn it over. Cover the bottom side with the right coloured icing - butter icing is best.
For Mice: plain butter cream, pink smartie eyes, a brown nose, liquorice tail and whiskers and white chocolate Buttons ears (or coat it with coloured almond paste).

Ladybirds: red butter cream and plain choc chip spots

Hedgehogs: Chocolate buttercream, cut chocolate Buttons in half and cover with these sticking up and 3 currants for eyes and a little nose.
I've given you starters for 10 - off you go kids!

Boiled Fruit Cake

This is my Harvest time tea cake. The big plus of this cake is that it is ready to eat as soon as it is cooked and cool. It is instantly moist and juicy, and it packs well to carry up the field or on the picnic!

Ingredients:

340 g Plain Flour
2tsp Baking Powder
1/2 tsp Bicarbonate of Soda
170 g Margarine or Butter
100g Soft Brown Sugar
1 tsp Mixed Spice
2 Eggs
225ml. Water
340g Dried Fruit
170gGolden Syrup

Method:

1. Boil together the water, margarine or butter, sugar, fruit and syrup. Gently simmer for 5 minutes and then allow to cool.

2. Sieve together the dry ingredients in a large bowl.

3. Beat the eggs in a separate bowl.

4. Once the fruit mixture has cooled beat all the ingredients together in the flour bowl and place in a lined 8" tin. Cook.

Aga in the baking oven for about an hour on the bottom set of runners, or in a cake baker on the floor of the roasting oven for about an hour.

Electric fan oven at 140°c (Gas mark 2) for 1 hour 45 minutes

Fruity and Herby Oils and Vinegars

While herbs and fresh fruits are plentiful, plan ahead for the Autumn and for Christmas presents (the cards must be in the shops by now)! Make herb oils and vinegars, which will immediately give a different dimension to any dish.

Herb Vinigar Ingredients:

500ml. Wine vinegar
or distilled vinegar
25-30 g Chopped fresh herbs -
Tarragon, Rosemary, Thyme, Sage
or Chives

Method:

1. Slowly warm the vinegar.

2. Lightly chop the chosen herb and place in a sterile jar.

3. Pour over the vinegar. Put on a non corrosive lid and shake. Keep at room temperature, shaking occasionally for two weeks.

4. Strain the vinegar through a sieve lined with kitchen paper, and bottle in a pretty bottle. Place a fresh sprig of the herb in the bottle. This is so that you know which herb it is and it also looks attractive if it is going to be a present.

5. The vinegar will keep for 6 months if stored in the dark.

Chilli Oil Ingredients:

4 Dried chillies or 6 fresh
3/4 tsp. Chilli powder
500ml. Olive oil

Method:

1. Put the oil, chillies and powder in a saucepan. Bring it slowly to the boil and then simmer very gently for 20 minutes. This can be done in the simmering oven of the Aga.

2. Take from the heat and pour into a clean bowl and leave covered with cling film for 3 days.

3. Strain through a sieve lined with kitchen paper and pour into a sterile bottle. Add two new dried chillies and seal. Four cloves of garlic can be added if you like.

4. This will keep for 6 months in a cool dark place.

   You could also make a garlic oil. Use six chopped cloves of garlic with the oil and then add fresh whole ones when bottling. Prepare it in the same way as the Chilli Oil.

Raspberry Vinegar
Ingredients:

500ml White wine vinegar
300g Fresh raspberries
2 tsp Caster sugar

Method:

1. Slowly warm the vinegar.

2. Gently crush the raspberries and place in a jar.

3. Pour over the warm vinegar. Put on a non corrosive lid and shake.

4. Store at room temperature for two weeks, shaking occasionally.

5. Strain through a kitchen paper lined sieve and put in a sauce pan with the sugar.

6. Heat until the sugar has dissolved then bottle in a clean bottle.

7. You can add about six perfect raspberries to the bottle if you like. Then seal the bottle. Store the vinegar in the dark and it keeps for 6 months.

September

September is Harvest Home time, so there are lots of fruit and vegetables to cook with and preserve. A time for warming, rich meat dishes and filling puds!

RECIPES

Fresh Vegetable Soup

Duck breast with Elderberry or Pork chops

Venison steaks with blackberries

Beef and Venison casserole

Roast Vegetables

Roast Vegetables in bread tartlets

Cornish Pasties

Vegetable Cornish pasty

Cornish Apple Cake

Jellies

Apple Jelly

Apple and Mint

Apple and Ginger

Apple and Elderberry

Damson Jelly

Grapefruit and Apple Curd

Fitton Chutney

Beetroot Chutney

Autumn Chutney

Strawberry Jam

Scones, Sweet and Savoury

Cookie Factory

Best Ever Triple Chocolate Pudding

Apple and Elderberry bread and butter pud

Fresh Vegetable Soup

Soup can so often be a meal in itself. It's so easy at this time of the year to use the surplus from the garden or what you fancy from the market or the shop shelves. Cut the pieces the size to suit your meal, whether it's a hearty lunch or snack, or a starter for supper or pop it all in the liquidizer for a smooth soup. Serve it with a swirl of cream and fresh herbs, crispy bacon bits or seeds sprinkled on the top. All these options to suit you can be adapted from one basic recipe! This is the basic recipe which you add and subtract from to suit what you like and what you have available.

Ingredients:

2tbs. Oil
1 Onion, chopped
4 Carrots, sliced
1 Small turnip or a small piece of swede, cut up into chunks
2 Sticks of celery, sliced
1 Red pepper, cut up
1 Potato, cubed
2 Cloves of garlic, crushed
1 tsp Mustard seed
Salt and pepper
1½ litres Vegetable stock
12 French beans, cut in two
8 Florets of cauliflower
1 Leek, sliced
6 Small tomatoes, halved
2 Handfuls chopped cabbage
30g Uncooked Pasta or 2 tbs cooked black eyed beans or similar
2 tbs. Chopped herbs - I like parsley.
2 Bay leaves
Parmesan or a tasty local cheese to grate over the soup

Method:

1. Wash, peel and prepare the vegetables cutting them into similar sized pieces.

2. Heat the oil in a large pan and add the onion, carrot, turnip or swede, celery, pepper and potato and cook for 5 minutes.

3. Add the garlic, mustard seed, salt and pepper and cook for a few more minutes. Add the stock and bring it to the boil.

4. Add the French beans, cauliflower, leek and tomatoes, bay leaves and 1 tbs of the chopped herbs and simmer gently for 20 minutes.

5. Add the cabbage and the pasta and cook for 10 minutes.

6. Remove the bay leaves. At this point if you want to liquidize it do so and then stir in the rest of the herbs.

7. Serve with your favourite cheese on top or separately - just in case it isn't everybody else's favourite! It's also delicious with hunks of home made bread.

Breast of Duck with Elderberry Sauce

Ingredients:

4 Duck Breasts - off the bone
100 ml Red wine
1 Small onion, chopped
1 Carrot
1 Clove of garlic
6 Juniper berries crushed
Fresh black pepper and salt
A little grated nutmeg
A sprig of parsley, sage and thyme
180ml   Stock
2 tbsElderberry Jelly (See following
recipe) blackcurrant or redcurrant
can be used instead
1 tbs Cassis or Port
Salt and Pepper

Method:

1. To make the marinade: chop the onion, carrot, garlic and the herbs. Add the red wine and seasonings. Marinade the duck breasts for at least 3 hours or overnight if you wish.

2. Remove the duck breasts and dry thoroughly. Slash the skin and fat in several places, taking care not to pierce the flesh.

3. Heat a small heavy frying pan and put in the meat, skin side down. Let it cook for 5 - 8 minutes and drain off the fat. Turn the meat and cook on the underside until done to your liking. The duck breasts take a surprisingly long time to cook; 12 - 15 minutes will still give pink meat.

4. Meanwhile heat the stock and the marinade in a small saucepan and reduce by two-thirds. Stir in the elderberry jelly.

5. Transfer the meat, when cooked, to a warm place to let it relax.

6. Skim any remaining fat from the
    frying pan and add the marinade.
    Boil it up, add the cassis or port
    and season to taste, if you want
    to the sauce can be strained
    before serving.

7. Spoon the sauce onto the
    heated plate and place the duck
    in the centre with the rest of the
    sauce served separately.

9. This is a rich dish so it only
    needs simple accompaniments -
    plain potatoes, or even pasta
    with a salad or green beans,
    sugar snaps, peas or broccoli.

    Pork chops can be cooked in the
    same way, the marinade give a
    darker almost gamely look to the
    pork. You can add a little seedy
    mustard to the sauce for this.

Venison Steaks

The marinade for the duck could be used for Venison steaks with 2 tbs of olive oil added, as venison is a very lean meat and can be dry, it is excellent if you are watching the choleserol level. Once you have taken the steaks out of the marinade, reduce the marinade in a saucepan. Cook the steaks quickly in a hot grill pan. If you like, just as the steaks are cooked you could add 2-3 tbs of brandy to the pan and flambè the steaks. Remove the steaks from the pan. Add some water to the pan to loosen the pan juices as best you can. Add these to the marinade in the saucepan with a 100g of freshly picked blackberries, heat through and stir as little as possible so as not to break up the berries too much.   Add 20g of butter to the sauce and let this melt into the sauce to give it a nice sheen. Check the seasoning, pour the sauce over the steaks and enjoy.

This is a delicious way to serve tender venison, if you have tougher meat try the stew recipe that follows.

Beef and Venison Casserole

A good game stew. The prunes could be replaced with apricots and the chestnuts could be walnuts! The cooking time depends on the meat and also how chunky you want the meat cut up. Jacket potatoes go well with this - let the oven take all the strain!

Ingredients:

500g Braising Steak - cut into large dice
500 g Venison - cut into large dice
2 tbs Flour
Oil and Butter for frying
Zest and Juice of 1 Oranges
3 Onions - chopped
500g Carrots - chopped
6 sticks Celery - sliced
2 tbs Tomato Puree
3 Cloves Garlic - crushed
11/2 litres Good Beef Stock
100 ml. Port or Madeira
200 g Cooked and peeled chestnuts
250g Ready to eat, pitted prunes
Lots of chopped parsley to serve

Method:

1. Put the oil and butter into the large pan to melt.

2. Toss the beef and venison in the flour and add to the oil and butter. Stir round well and seal the meat.

3. After 5 minutes take out the meat and put it in a casserole dish. Add the onion, celery and carrot to the pan. Add a little more oil if needed and cook for 5-10 minutes.

4. Add all the other ingredients to the meat, apart from the chestnuts and prunes. Bring the contents to the boil, simmer for 10 minutes and then place in the oven and cook for 2-3 hours until tender.

5. **Aga** in the simmering oven

   Electric fan oven at 140ºc (Gas mark 2)
   If you have a bottom heat facility in your oven use this at 180ºc, stirring occasionally.

6. An hour before the end of cooking add the chestnuts and prunes, stir well and continue cooking.

   Serve with creamy mashed potato and crisp green vegetables.

Roasted Vegetables and Vegetable Tartlets

Ingredients:

Vegetable oil
A selection of vegetables:
Assorted Peppers, Red Onions,
Fennel, Parsnips, Carrots, Celery,
Aubergine, Courgette, hunks of
peeled Squash or Kumera the
choice is yours!
1 tbs Soy sauce
1 tbs Balsamic Vinegar
2 tsp Root ginger, grated
2 cloves of garlic, crushed
Salt and pepper

Method:

1. In a roasting tin heat the oil - put
   this in the oven to get really hot.
   Cut the vegetables into even
   sized pieces and toss these in
   the hot oil. Place in the oven and
   cook for about 20 minutes.
   Aga: cook in the roasting oven

   Electric fan oven at 180°C
   (Gas mark 7)

2. Remove from the oven and add
   the soy sauce, balsamic vinegar,
   garlic, root ginger and salt and
   pepper.

3. Pour these over the vegetables,
   give them a good stir and place
   in the oven for another 10- 20
   minutes.

4. Serve as vegetables or cold as a
   salad with a little extra oil.

5. To serve the vegetables in crispy
   bread tartlets as a starter: cut the
   vegetables smaller and cook in
   the same way for a shorter time.
   Then cube some cheese add
   this with some chopped fresh
   herbs to the tartlets.

Crispy bread tartlets
Ingredients:
12 slices of bread
60 mls. Salted Butter
1 tsp. paprika

Method:

1. Melt the butter with the paprika.

2. Cut the crusts off the bread and
   roll flat with a rolling pin. Brush
   each side of the bread with the
   butter and press into deep muffin
   tins to form the tartlets.

3. **Aga** in the roasting oven on the
   grid shelf on the floor of the oven
   for 10 minutes.

   Electric fan oven at 180°C
   (Gas mark 7) until golden brown.

4. Remove from the tins and fill with
   the vegetable and cheese mix
   just before you serve them.

Cornish Pasties

This is a recipe shared with me when I was down in Cornwall doing some demonstrations at St. Austell. I'm afraid I haven't got the lady's name, but it is a recipe that had been in her family for generations.

Short Crust Pastry Ingredients:

500 g Plain flour
160g Lard or vegetable shortening
120g Margarine or butter
1 tsp. salt
6 tbs. water

Method:

1. Place all the ingredients, except the water, in a food processor and whiz to breadcrumbs. Add to enough water to give a firm, but not sticky, pastry.

2. Allow to rest in the refrigerator.

The Pasties:

Equal amounts of: beef skirt, potato, swede and onion with salt and pepper and butter or suet to moisten.

Method:

1. The ingredients can either be cut into even fairly small cubes and seasoned really well with salt and pepper or the vegetables can be chopped very finely or grated and the meat cut up finely too, this way they cook quicker.

2. Roll out the pastry and cut out 20cm rounds around a plate or use a flan dish as a cutter.

3. Put a reasonable amount of filling on one half. Fold over the other half and fold the edges together, pressing down gently with your finger to giving a twist effect as you go. Brush with egg wash if you like a glazed finish and cook.

Aga on the floor of the roasting oven for 20-30 minutes. Put the cold shelf on the second set of runners if they are browning too quickly or move to the simmering oven for 20 minutes to finish cooking depending on the size.

Electric fan oven at 180°c (Gas mark 7) for 10 minutes then reduce the temperature to 160°c (Gas mark 5) for a further 40-50 minutes.

When they were working down the mines they had a pasty with savoury at one end and sweet at the other end - the perfect packed lunch! Try equal quantities of grated apple and fresh breadcrumbs, with a pinch of cinnamon,a tsp. of raisins and soft brown sugar, the breadcrumbs absorb the juice - an interesting combination! See picture above.

Vegetable Pasties

Instead of the meat you can,have 60g. each of potato, swede, onion , mushroom carrot, 1 tbs chopped parsley and lots of salt and pepper.Chop the onion and mushroom and grate the rest, and cook for just 15 minutes.

Another alternative is red cabbage, potato and caraway seed with some mixed herbs.

Cornish Apple Cake

This recipe idea was sown in the West Country and adapted - it's great for using windfall apples, which won't keep. In the recipe you can add all sultanas and no ginger (whatever dried fruit is in the cupboard) and add 1 teaspoon of either ground cinnamon or mixed spice.

Ingredients:

170g Margarine or butter
170g Soft brown sugar or caster sugar
3 Eggs
400g Cooking apples, peeled, cored and grated
300g Self raising flour
100g Glace ginger
180g Sultanas
1 tsp Ground ginger

Topping:

150g Plain flour
100g Butter
60g Demerara or granulated sugar
1 tsp Ground ginger

Method:

1. Make the topping in the processor. Put the flour, butter and ground ginger in the bowl and process to breadcrumbs. Just pulse in the sugar, until it starts to stick together in crumbly lumps and remove from the bowl.

2. Grate the apple - I do this in the processor too!

3. Beat together the margarine and sugar and add the eggs one at a time. Then fold in the rest of the ingredients.
Put the mixture in a greased 25 cm. spring clip tin and bake.

4. **Aga** on the bottom set of runners in the baking oven for about an hour, or in a lined 20 cm tin in the cake baker on the floor of the roasting oven for about 1¹/4 hours, remove the lid for the last 10 mins to brown the crumble a bit more.

Electric fan oven at 150°c (Gas mark 4) for about an hour and 15 minutes Cook in a combination oven at 160°c with 180 watt microwave for only 25-30 minutes

5. Allow to cool. Serve dusted with icing sugar.

To get the cake out of the cake baker tin: allow to cool and then run a knife between the liner and the tin to loosen. Cover the top of the cake and the tin with cling film and turn the cake out onto a plate upside down. Then with the help of the cling film turn it the right way up, removing the lining paper as you do so. Dust with icing sugar.

Jellies

Once the winds start blowing and the apples start falling off the trees, it is the time to start making jelly. The crab apples usually ripen first and give a wonderful pinky orange jelly with a really sharp flavour. Crab apple jelly is excellent on its own. Ordinary cooking apples make a good agent for other flavours to be added to. Do be careful when preparing the apples to discard any bruised fruit as it can affect the flavour if it is starting to ferment. So get out that preserving pan and let's get cracking. It is so satisfying as the jam jars fill up with jellies, jams and chutneys!

Apple Jelly

The basic apple jelly can have all sorts of ingredients added, see below:

Ingredients:

Apples.
Enough water to cover
10 cm root ginger
Or 10 cloves
Or 20 cm Cinnamon stick
Or the juice and pared rind of lemon, lime or orange
Or a good bunch of mint or any other herb
Methylated spirit to check pectin content

Method:

1. Wash and check the apples, removing any bruised bits. Quarter any large apples.

2. Put the apples in the preserving pan and just cover with water (1½ litres to 2 kilos of fruit, approximately). Add the fresh flavourings that you want to add.

3. Bring to the boil and simmer gently to soften the fruit and extract the pectin (in the Aga simmering oven).

4. Strain the fruit pulp through a scalded jelly bag and let it drain. Don't squeeze the juice out as this makes the jelly cloudy.

5. If the syrup seems thin, boil it and reduce it slightly.

6. You can do a **pectin test** as follows: Put a teaspoon of the juice in a glass and add 3 tsp of methylated spirit. Shake it gently together and leave it to set for a minute. Then pour it out of the glass. If it comes out in one lump there is plenty of pectin. If it separates into two lumps the pectin is fair, but if it breaks up into lots of bits the pectin content is low. The higher the pectin content the better the juice will set. Apples are usually reasonably high in pectin.

7. If the pectin content seems low, boil the juice up and reduce and try the test again.

8. Measure the juice and to every 550 ml of juice you can add 450g of sugar. I use granulated sugar. I always have some in the cupboard, so can make jelly any time. Preserving sugar, however, sometimes has pectin in and can give a sparklier finish.

9. Warm the sugar, this helps it dissolve more quickly. Bring the juice to the boil (Aga in the roasting oven) and add the measured amount of sugar. The golden rule of Jam and Jelly Making is slow cooking before the addition of the sugar and very rapid and short cooking afterwards.

10. Stir continually until the sugar is dissolved and then boil rapidly to setting point on the hob. I have a sugar thermometer which takes all the guess work out of deciding on setting point, simply boil to 106°c-110°c reading on the thermometer - it will probably say jam there! Otherwise put a small amount on a cold saucer put it in the refrigerator allow to go cold and push the jelly with your finger if it wrinkles it is ready to pot!

12. With a large spoon skim off excessive foam or scum while boiling. Put the spoon in a jug of water between skimmings to keep the jelly clear. A walnut size piece of butter added to the jelly also helps to disperse the foam.

13. When setting point is reached, take the pan from the heat and place on a damp dishcloth to stop the cooking. The jelly can now be potted in clean warm jars.

Apple and Mint Jelly

Ingredients:

A bunch of mint
2 tbs. Freshly chopped mint
Green colouring , otherwise it is a pale browny colour!
150 ml. Vinegar, malt, cider or wine

Method:

1. Add the bunch of mint and vinegar to the apples as they are simmered to give flavour to the juice.

2. Add the chopped mint and some green colouring, if you want to, to the boiling jelly just before setting point.

3. Let the jelly stand for a few minutes to prevent all the mint rising to the top of the jar.

Apple and Ginger Jelly

Ingredients:

2 Pieces of fresh root ginger
Glace ginger or stem ginger in syrup

Method:

1. Crush a reasonable piece of ginger and add to the apples as they cook.

2. Add some peeled and finely chopped fresh root ginger or the glace ginger or finely chopped stem ginger to the boiling jelly just before setting point.

3. Let the jelly rest again and stir well before potting.

PAM'S
MARMALADE

Passion
Fr

Strawberry

int Jelly
Sept. '01

fitton Chutne
Sept '01

EMON
CURD

Apple and Elderberry Jelly

Ingredients:

1¹/₂kg Apples
1¹/₂kg Elderberries
Juice of 1 lemon
Sugar 340g to each 550ml of juice
A few cloves

Method:

1. Slowly cook the apples and the elderberries in separate saucepans just covered with water. With the juice of the lemon added to the elderberries until tender. Add 10-12 cloves to the apples if you like the flavour. It's a good addition because the jelly can be used in meat sauces and served with hot and cold meats and pâtés.

2. Strain the juice through a jelly bag and mix the juices together. Test the pectin and reduce the juice if necessary.

3. Measure the juice and warm the sugar as the juices come to the boil, (Aga do this on the floor of the roasting oven) add the sugar and stir until the sugar is dissolved.

4. Boil quickly to setting point on the hob or boiling plate.

5. Remove from the heat and pot in warm jars and cover.

Damson Jelly

This recipe is here because I hail from Cheshire and there are a lot of Damson trees in Cheshire. Damsons are a small, dark and very delicious plum, which is high in pectin. Mum made some very stiff Damson jam and it was excellent for packed sandwiches. We used to have a damson jam and crumbly Cheshire cheese filling. I can taste it now - it was an excellent combination and the jam never ran out of the sandwich! I prefer to make jelly as there are an awful lot of stones to skim off if you make jam. A few always escaped which were great for tinker, tailor, soldier, sailor, rich man, poor man, beggar man, thief! Who would one marry, count the stones!
Damson jelly is a good substitute for glazing tarts and in the bottom of tarts such as Bakewells and is wonderful on scones with clotted cream!

Ingredients:

2¹/2 kilo Damsons
1¹/2 litres Water
450g Sugar to each 550 ml of juice

Method:

1. Wash and check the fruit. Put it in the preserving pan with the water and cook it slowly to soften the fruit and extract the pectin.

2. Strain through a jelly bag.

3. Measure the juice and weigh the appropriate amount of sugar. Warm the sugar. Bring the juice to the boil (Aga do this on the floor of the roasting oven) and boil quickly to setting point.

4. Remove from the heat, pot and cover in warm jars.

Do try damson jelly and Cheshire cheese sandwiches!

Grapefruit and Apple Curd

Ingredients:

400g Cooking Apples
120 g Butter
220 g Sugar
1 Grapefruit
2 Eggs

Method:

1. Wash, quarter and core the apples.

2. Cook in a saucepan with 2 tbs water or in the microwave at 600-watt for 5-10 minutes until bursting and fluffy. Sieve to give a puree.

3. Put the butter, sugar, grapefruit rind and juice in a large bowl. Melt in the simmering oven, or cook at 600 watt for 2 minutes in the microwave to melt ingredients together. Add the apple.

4. Strain in the beaten eggs and mix well in.

5. Cook over a pan of boiling water to a creamy curd.
   Or at 360 Watts in the microwave for 2 minutes. Stir well and keep cooking on half power in the microwave for a minute at a time until a thick creamy curd consistency is reached.

6. Pot and label.
   Keeps for 6 weeks in a refrigerator.

Fitton Chutney

This is Mum's Chutney that I grew up enjoying - I hope you do too. It is a very old recipe, and it goes back to Queen Elizabeth the First!

Ingredients:

1 kilo Apples
1 kilo Tomatoes, skinned & chopped
6-7 Onions, chopped
450 g Soft brown Sugar
300g Raisins
2 tbs. Salt
1 tps. Cayenne Pepper
1 litre Malt Vinegar

Method:

1. Peel and core the apples. Roughly chop them, place them in saucepan, and cover them with vinegar.

2. Bring the vinegar to the boil and simmer for 5 minutes.

3. Add the tomatoes and remaining vinegar and boil to a pulp. This can be done in the roasting oven of the Aga

4. Chop the onions and add with raisins to the vinegar, apple and tomato mix with all the other ingredients. Bring to the boil and simmer gently for about 1/2 an hour (in the simmering oven of the Aga) and bottle.

Beetroot Chutney

Ingredients:

1¹/₂kg Cooked Beetroot
800ml. Vinegar
2 Medium Onions
Rind and Juice of 1 Lemon
600g Cooking apples
350g Soft brown sugar
1 tsp Ground ginger
Salt

Method:

1. Chop the cooked beetroot finely.

2. Peel, core and chop the apples and the onion. Place in a saucepan.

3. Add sugar, vinegar, seasonings, lemon rind and juice and simmer until tender.

4. Add the beetroot and simmer for a further 15 minutes. If too runny reduce further.

5. Pot and cover.
   Keeps for 6 months.

Autumn Chutney

Ingredients:

1kg Mixed Autumn Produce (e.g.
Plums, Tomatoes, Red and Green
Apples and Courgettes)
300g Onions (Sliced)
1 tsp Ground Ginger
$1/2$ tsp Coriander
$1/2$ tsp Cayenne
$1/2$ tsp Cinnamon
300ml Malt Vinegar
300g Dark Brown Sugar

Method:

1. Wash, peel and chop the fruit.
   Mix with all the ingredients in a
   large bowl, or preserving pan.

2. If using a microwave loosely
   cover the bowl with a plate or
   microwave film and microwave
   on 600 watt for 15 minutes,
   stirring 2 or 3 times until the
   sugar has dissolved.

3. Remove the cover and cook at
   600 watt for 35 minutes.

4. If using an **Aga** cook on the floor
   of the roasting oven in the
   preserving pan for 30 minutes
   and then move to the simmering
   oven to soften the fruit even
   more.

5. If it needs reducing further return
   to the roasting oven for 15
   minutes or until the right
   consistency is reached.

6. Pour into clean, warm, dry jars
   and seal.

Strawberry Jam

A Speedy method for a big pot of jam in a hurry

Ingredients:

450g Strawberries
The juice of a lemon
340g Sugar

Method:

1   Place the fruit in a large bowl.
    Add the lemon juice, cover and
    cook at 700W for approximately
    5 - 10 minutes, or until the fruit
    is soft.

2   Stir in the sugar and cook
    uncovered for 15 - 20 minutes or
    until the setting point is reached.
    Stir the jam regularly during
    cooking, at 700 watt in
    the microwave.

3   To test the setting point: Pour a
    little jam onto a cold saucer and
    leave for a minute. A skin should
    form on top of the jam, which
    wrinkles when touched.

4   Allow the jam to cool before
    pouring into clean, dry jars.
    Cover with a waxed disc and lid.

Scones

I like this recipe best as you don't have that awful baking powder taste sticking to your teeth! The dough is best slightly soft. You can make the scones richer by adding an egg, but I think this is unnecessary - scones should be simple. If you have any sour milk this is an excellent way of using it up as it makes incredibly light scones!

Ingredients:

225g Plain Flour
1 tsp Bicarbonate of Soda
2 tsp Cream of Tartar
Pinch of Salt
40g Butter
150ml Milk

Sweet Scones
 Add 1 tbs. Sugar to the mix

Ginger Scones
Add 50 g Glace ginger
and $1/2$ tsp. ground ginger with the sugar

Cheese Scones
Add 100g Grated cheese
1/2 tsp. Dry mustard
Pinch of Cayenne

Method:

1   Sieve the dry ingredients into a large bowl and rub in the butter.

2   Add the milk and cut with a knife very quickly together to form a moist, light dough.(I'm not sure why I wrote that, I always do them in the Magimix or Kitchen Aid!!)

3   Roll carefully out and cut into circles. (Fluted cutter for sweet and a plain cutter for savoury scones!)

4   Sometimes though if you are making dried fruit scones you get a better finish with a plain cutter as there is less edge to drag the fruit down as you cut them out. This is another piece of fairly useless information - but not a lot of people know that!

5   Place these on the Bake-o-Glide lined baking sheet and cook.

Aga on the cold shelf as a baking sheet and cook in the roasting oven for about 10 minutes on the bottom set of runners.

Electric fan oven at 180°c (Gas mark 7) for 10- 15 minutes

6   Allow to cool and then cut in half and decorate.

7   If you are making sweet scones - clotted cream and homemade jam are wonderful or just buttered

8   If you are making cheesy scones you can also add chopped herbs and chilli or curry powder. Make them small and they make wonderful bases for savouries.

9   They can be topped with a combination of cream cheese and butter beaten together and piped on top. You can then finish them with a couple of prawns, a twirl of smoked salmon, a little caviar, half a grape, a strawberry, a little egg, cherry tomato or cucumber - the variations are endless.

Cookie Factory
Double Choc Chip Cookies

Ingredients:

225 g Margarine or butter
115g Soft Brown Sugar
110gCaster Sugar
2 Eggs
1 tsp. Bicarbonate of Soda
280g Plain Flour
1 tps. Salt
40 g Cocoa powder
40 g Chopped Nuts
100 g Plain chocolate chips
100 g White chocolate chips
1 tsp. Vanilla Essence

Method:

1. Cream the butter and sugar. Beat in the eggs.

2. Add the bicarbonate of soda, flour, cocoa, salt, chopped nuts, choc chips and vanilla essence. Mix in well.

3. This mixture is best left to chill overnight in the refrigerator. The mixture will keep for two weeks in the refrigerator. It is ready for cooking at a moment's notice, or it can be frozen.

4. Put teaspoons of the mixture on the lined baking tray about 10cm apart and cook.

Aga on a Bake-o-Glide lined cold shelf. Flatten slightly and put on the grid shelf on the floor of the roasting oven for 8-12 minutes or in the baking oven on the bottom set of runners for 20 minutes

Electric fan oven 160ºC
(Gas mark 5) for 10-20 minutes

5 Remove while still warm to a cooling rack, store in an airtight tin.

Cookie Factory:

Possible Ingredients Changes to the main Double Chocolate Chip Recipe

Peanut Cookies

Omit: the cocoa powder and the chocolate chips
Add: 2 tbs peanut butter
and 1 extra tbs plain flour.

Cherry & Coconut

Omit: the cocoa powder, nuts and chocolate chips.
Add: 150g Chopped glace cherries and 80g desiccated coconut

Raisin & Lemon

Omit: the cocoa powder and chocolate chips, the nuts can be left in, you decide!
Add: the zest of 2 lemons
and 2 tbs. of juice and 100 g Raisins or sultanas and 1 tsp mixed spice .

Cinnamon & Papaya

Omit: thecocoa powder and the chocolate chips.
Add: 100g crystallized papaya and 1 tsp ground cinnamon.

Ginger

Omit: the cocoa powder and the chocolate chips and the nuts.
Add: 100 g Glace ginger
and 1 tsp. ground ginger.

Pecan & Maple

Omit: the chocolate chips and 60 g of castor sugar.
Add: 1 tbs maple syrup and 100g chopped pecan nuts, these can be sprinkled with demerara sugar before cooking.

Macadamia & white chocolate

Omit: the cocoa powder and the plain chocolate chips.
Add: 100g Macadamia halves.

The list could go on so add your own ideas, let production begin!

227

Best Ever Triple Chocolate Pudding

There is something very comforting about hot chocolate steamed puds. According to you good people out there who have tasted it at demonstrations, this is my best ever.

Ingredients:

120g Butter
120g Soft brown sugar
2 large Eggs
150g Self raising flour
25g Cocoa powder
25g Fresh breadcrumbs
50g White chocolate chips
50g Plain chocolate chips
1/2 tsp. Bicarbonate of soda
4 tbs. Brandy or your favourite liqueur

Sauce:

150 g Plain chocolate
50 g Butter
4tbs. Brandy or that liqueur or water

Method:

1. Cream the butter and sugar and add the eggs one at a time, beating really well.

2. Add all the other ingredients, mix gently and thoroughly together.

3. Grease and base line at least a 1 litre size bowl. Put the mixture in this and cover with a lid or pleated double foil over the top. If using foil, fold the edges under the rim of the bowl. Cook.

4. **Aga:** Put a large saucepan with 6cm of water to boil. Put a trivet in the bottom of the pan to lift the bowl off the base. (Folded newspaper will do, it gets a bit soggy and falls apart, but it does the job!) Lower the bowl into the water and put the lid on the pan. Cook on the floor of the roasting oven for 15-30 minutes Then move to the simmering oven for 11/2- 2 hrs.to finish cooking, although it comes to no harm if left for longer!

Microwave: Cover the pudding bowl with cling film and pierce this to let out the steam. Cook for 10 minutes at 600 watts. Allow to rest before turning out

5. Turn the pudding out onto a warm serving dish. Pour a little sauce over the pud and serve the rest separately-Enjoy!

The Sauce:

Melt the sauce ingredients together on the back of the Aga or in the microwave at 360 watt for 3-4 minutes.
Then whisk together until smooth and glossy.

Apple and Elderberry Bread and Butter Pudding

They have become a habit these puds! You can use blackberries instead of the elderberries. Either way there is something nice about raiding the hedgerows for the filling!

Ingredients:

8-12 rounds of bread and butter
2 Large cooking apples
100 g Elderberries or blackberries - washed
Juice of a lemon
100gDemerara sugar
1 tsp. Ground cinnamon
2 Eggs
300 mls. Single cream

Method:

1. Butter an ovenproof dish and line with the bread and butter.

2. Peel and chop the apples and toss in the lemon juice.

3. Mix the cinnamon with the demerara.

4. Shake any excess lemon juice off the apple and mix with the elderberries.

5. Put a layer of the fruit over the first layer of bread and butter and sprinkle with the sugar mix. Put a layer of bread and butter on top and then more fruit.

6. Beat the cream and eggs together. Pour over the pudding and sprinkle over the remaining sugar mix just before cooking. Allow to stand for at least 30 minutes before cooking.

To cook:

Aga on the grid shelf on the floor of
the roasting oven for 25- 35 minutes.
If it is browning too quickly, put the
cold shelf above.

Electric fan oven at 160°c (Gas
mark 5) for 30- 40 minutes.

October

Halloween, falling leaves, bonfires, damp, darkening days, warming casseroles of pheasant and lamb, with fruity suet pudding - comfort food to the fore!

RECIPES

Pumpkin Dip

Fish and Avocado Layers with Trout

Pheasant Pie

Pheasant with Cranberries and Ginger

Slow Cooked Lamb with Prunes

Rosemary Potatoes

Choux Swans

Praline

Choux Savoury Puff and Profiteroles

Gougere of Fish, Game or Vegetables

Cheese Pastry Bats and Things

Bramble Suet Pudding

Cox's and Calvados

Totally Nutty Bread and Butter Pud

Auntie Nan's Ginger Biscuits

Excellent Christmas Cake

Trick or Treat Treacle Toffee

Pumpkin Dip

There are lots of pumpkins about in October. With Halloween at the end of the month, they provide a different way to cook and serve a dip and this recipe is great for a Halloween party. You also have a cooked vegetable or the basis of a soup left over as a bonus! The mixture is delicious served on toast. I have had this on more than one occasion whilst writing this book! The choice of cheese and what you add to the cheese is up to you. I often have just cheese, a little finely chopped onion and a couple of tablespoons of cream or milk, cooked in the simmering oven till melted and poured on bread or toast. It's funny how you remember odd things - I remember Uncle Clifford, (whose farm the cheese had been made on!) taking an enamel plate out of the simmering oven of his Aga with this mixture on. I think it had been in there for quite some time. It tasted delicious - I was about ten the time, a long time ago!

Ingredients:

1 Small Pumpkin
300g Strong flavoured cheese, grated
2 tbs Finely chopped chives, or Spring onions
1 Clove of garlic, crushed
2 tsp Mustard powder
Salt and pepper
A Dash of Worcestershire sauce or Tabasco sauce
100ml Cream any type even soured

Method:

1. Cut the top off the pumpkin and scoop out all the seeds. Save the top as a lid.

2. Mix the cheese, mustard powder, herbs, garlic and seasonings and then add the cream.

3. Pour this into the pumpkin, do not over fill the pumpkin , it may overflow! replace the lid and put in the oven to cook, in a tin or dish.

4. Once cooked, the dip just needs a stir and a few fresh chopped herbs sprinkled on the top.

5. Pass the pumpkin around with crisps, cheesy bats (see later recipe) and vegetable sticks to dip in the dip!

Aga: Place the pumpkin on the grid shelf on the bottom set of runners in the baking oven for about 1 hour. Or in the roasting oven on the grid shelf on the floor of the roasting oven for 30 minutes Followed by as long as you like in the simmering oven!

Electric fan oven 160°c (Gas mark 5) for 1-2 hours

Once the dip has been eaten, the pumpkin flesh can be scooped out and mashed with some butter and pepper and served as a vegetable.

Alternatively the pumpkin flesh can be cooked with some onion, carrot and stock for a tasty pumpkin soup. Accompany this with lots of fresh herbs, grated cheese and crispy croutons.

The dip can be made in an ovenproof pot instead of the pumpkin. Cook in the Aga in the simmering oven for 30 minutes approximately. Cook in a microwave oven at 360 watts for 4-6 minutes.

Fish and Avocado Layers with Trout

Serves 8

Ingredients:

2 Cooked trout fillets

Fish mousse:

100 g Cooked prawns or smoked salmon bits
100ml Fsh stock
2 tsp Powdered gelatine
150 ml. Mayonnaise
1 tbs Tomato puree
A good dash of Tabasco
Salt and a pinch of sugar to taste

Avocado mousse:

2 Avocado
1 Clove garlic, crushed
1 tbs Chopped chives
1 tbs Chopped basil
Juice of a lemon
2 tsp Powdered gelatine
2 tbs Water
200 g Cream cheese
250 ml. Greek yogurt
Salt and pepper
Tomatoes for garnish

Method:

1. Add the gelatine to the fish stock. Allow it to sponge .

2. Let it melt on the back of the Aga or over a pan of water, or in the microwave at 360 watt for 1 minutes. Allow to cool slightly.

3. Line a 1 1/2-2 kg loaf tin with cling film.

4. Process the prawns or the smoked salmon. Add the seasonings and the mayonnaise and just pulse. With the motor running, slowly pour in the melted gelatine.

5. Pour the mixture into the lined tin. Allow this to set and then lay the fillets on top, head to tail.

6. To make the avocado mousse: Melt the gelatine and water as above.

7. Halve, stone and peel the avocados. Place in the processor with the lemon juice and the garlic and process. Add the cream cheese and herbs and then the gelatine, finally the yogurt and the seasoning.

8. Pour this carefully over the trout and allow to set. This will take about 4 hours, in the refridgerator.

9. To serve, turn out onto a serving dish. The cling film makes this very easy.

   Skin and quarter the tomatoes. Arrange these around the mousse and serve with melba toast.

Pheasant Pie

A great way to serve tough old birds! If the bird has big hard spurs, then you have an old bird!

Cook 2 Pheasants in a casserole with water, onions, carrots, celery and herbs, bring to the boil and cook for about 15 minutes on the top then put in the simmering oven of the Aga and leave until tender - this will depend on the age of the birds, or you can do this on the hob simmering very slowly, let the pheasant go cold in the casserole and remove from the liquid and then boil up the liquid and reduce to make a tasty stock.

Ingredients

1 or 2 cooked pheasant
1 Large Onion
225g Mushrooms
8 Rashers Streaky Bacon
90g Butter
80g Flour
200ml Milk
300g Strong Cheddar cheese
More herbs and seasoning
A packet of ready made puff pastry
1 egg for egg wash to glaze the pie

Method:

1. Chop the onion, the mushrooms and the bacon. Sauté these together, stirring occasionally. If the bacon is very lean, add a little oil or butter. Give these about 10 minutes until they have started to soften and take just a little colour.

2. Make a thick white sauce with the butter, flour and milk . Melt the butter in a large saucepan add the flour and stir to bind with the butter and cook for a minute and then add the milk a little at a time stirring continuosly until you have a cooked , smooth sauce. Add a little of the stock to give some flavour, about 50ml.

3. Add your favourite chopped herbs - in this case I like Parsley and Thyme. Add the grated cheese, mix well together. Check the seasoning. Butter a deep pie dish.

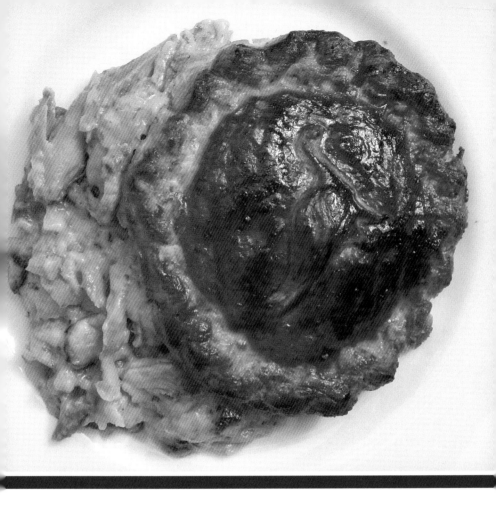

4. Remove the meat from the pheasants and cut it into large, bite size pieces. Mix these into the sauce with the onion, mushroom and bacon mix.

5. Place this in the dish and top with puff pastry. Brush with egg wash and cook.

Aga in the roasting oven for about 3/4 hour, depending on the depth of the pie - until the pastry is puffed and golden brown.

Electric fan oven at 170°c (Gas mark 6) for 45 -50 minutes. Serve - simple vegetables, mash and greens, go well with this dish.

Pheasant with Cranberries and Ginger

Ingredients:

2 Pheasants
2 Large garlic clove, crushed
1 tbs Finely chopped fresh root ginger
1 Onion, finely chopped
1 Orange, rind and juice
300ml Red wine
150g Cranberries
2tbs Apple jelly
2tbsp Tomato puree
2 Bay leaves
A sprig of parsley and thyme
Salt & pepper
2 tsp Cornflour

Method:

1. Place pheasants in a heat proof casserole and add the garlic, ginger, onion, a teaspoon of the orange rind and the cranberries.

2. Mix together the wine, orange juice, apple jelly and tomato puree. Pour this over the pheasants.

3. Add plenty of seasoning, cover and cook.
   Aga: Cook for 30 minutes in the roasting oven followed by 1-2 hours in the simmering oven until the pheasants are tender.
   Electric fan oven at 150°c (Gas mark 3) for 1 1/2- 2 hours.

4. Remove the pheasants from the casserole and joint them. Bone the joints and remove any shot. Keep the pheasant warm.

5. Strain the juices through a sieve and force through some of the fruit and vegetables. Reheat the sauce. Adjust the seasoning to taste and thicken the sauce with a tsp of cornflour if necessary.

6. Place the joints on a serving dish and pour the sauce over them. Tagliatelle and green vegetables look pretty with the pheasant and taste good too or just veg!

241

Slow Cooked Lamb with Prunes

This has been the most popular casserole that I do at demonstrations at the moment, so here's the recipe. I must admit that it is my favourite too. My butcher in Newport Pagnell sells me mutton to make this with, which has more flavour and long cooking allows the flavours to develop beautifully and makes the mutton deliciously tender.

Ingredients:

One Kilo Leg of Lamb - boned and cut into 5cms. cubes
4 tbs Olive Oil
2 Carrots
3 Cloves Garlic
3 Bay Leaves
150g Black Olives
150ml Beef Stock
50 g Flour
1 Onion
2 Stick of Celery
1 tbs Toasted Coriander Seeds
2 tbs Chopped Parsley (1 tbs to sprinkle for garnish)
250g Ready Soaked Prunes
200ml Red Wine

Method:

1. Dust the lamb with the flour. Heat the oil and seal the meat.

2. Place in the casserole dish.

3. Sauté the vegetables and then add to the meat. Add all the other ingredients, and bring to the boil. Cook until the meat is tender.

Aga on the floor of the roasting oven for 30 minutes followed by 1-2 hours in the simmering oven - of course it doesn't come to any harm if there for longer!

Electric fan oven: at 150°c (Gas mark 3) for 2 hours approximately.

4. When the meat is tender, sprinkle generously with chopped parsley, coriander or basil.

Serve with rice and a crisp well dressed salad. Enjoy!

Rosemary Potatoes

This is an all the year round recipe which is suitable for old and new potatoes. It goes with most of the dishes here. You can add other root vegetables if you like.

Ingredients:

450 g Potatoes cut into 2 cm dice
2 tbs Oil
4 Cloves Garlic
2 Sprigs Rosemary
Salt and Black Pepper

Method:

1. Put the oil in a small roasting tin.

2. Put the cubes of potato in water to soak for a little while to remove excess starch.

3. Remove from the water and dry thoroughly.

4. Toss the potatoes in the oil with the garlic, rosemary, sea salt and pepper and cook.

Aga in the roasting oven for about 3/4 hour until nice and crisp.

Electric in the fan oven at 180°c (Gas mark 7) for 30 -50 minutes.

Choux Swans

I can't remember how many years that I have been doing these for, but they keep coming back! They are fun and give me an opportunity to cover choux pastry which is so good for sweet and savoury dishes. This is the basic recipe.

Choux Pastry Ingredients:

60g Butter
150ml Water
70g Plain Flour
2 Eggs

For the Filling:

Cream and Fresh Fruit or Praline

Method:

1. Melt the butter with the water in a saucepan. Bring to the boil.

2. Remove from the heat. Add the flour and beat until the flour is just incorporated.

3. Beat the eggs in a bowl. allowing the flour mixture to cool slightly,

4. Add the egg mixture a little at a time. Beat it well in between each addition, to give a smooth, shiny paste.

5. Place in a piping bag with a plain nozzle. Pipe number 2 shapes onto a Bake-o-Glide lined cold shelf.

If you have a piece of almond you can use this to put a small sliver where the swan's beak would be - at the top of the 2 shape.
Shape the rest of the choux mix into even sized puffs - this amount makes 6 or 7 "swans".

6. To Cook
Aga: Place in the roasting oven.
Electric fan oven180°c
(Gas mark 7)
After 10 minutes remove the number 2 shapes and put these in the simmering oven to dry out completely. Leave the puffs in the roasting oven for a little longer till well risen, firm and golden brown. This will take between 20-30 minutes, depending on the size of the puffs. Remove the swans from the oven. Cut the puffs in half and place in the simmering oven or the warming oven for 20-30 minutes to dry out.

Turn off the electric or gas oven, but leave the cut puffs in the oven to dry out with the door slightly ajar(they will then keep for a day or two)

7. When the puffs are cold sandwich the two halves together with cream. Praline can be folded into the cream if you like.

8. Arrange some fresh fruit over the cream in the gap between the two puffs and slide the necks into position between the two halves with the choux standing up - and there is your Choux Swan!

9. You may dust them over with icing sugar or serve them with a chocolate sauce, depending if you want white or "black" swans.

Praline

Ingredients:

100g Whole almonds with skins still
on preferably
100g Caster sugar

Method:

1. Place the sugar and the nuts in a saucepan and heat on the simmering plate, over medium heat until they start to colour.

2. Transfer to the boiling plate or turn up the heat, stirring occasionally until they are a light golden brown.

3. Remove from the heat and put the base of the pan onto a damp dish cloth to stop it cooking.

4. Pour the mixture onto a sheet of bake-o-glide and leave to cool.

5. Break up the praline. Drop into a processor whilst it is running and process to a rough powder.

6. Store in a screw top jar until needed.

Choux Puffs or Profiteroles

Make up the choux pastry as before. Place in teaspoonfuls on a lined baking tray and cook for 15-20 minutes. Cut them half way through or make a hole to let out the steam. Allow them to dry out for 20 minutes in a cooler oven.

They can then be filled with whipped cream. Brandy and a little sugar can be added to the cream, alternatively add your favourite liqueur. Pile the choux in a pyramid and pour over chocolate sauce. (See September)

Savoury fillings make great little cocktail savouries. When cooking the puffs, sprinkle grated cheese, rock salt or finely chopped nuts or seeds over the raw paste. Here is a list of suggested fillings.

Add to Cream Cheese:-
Finely shredded ham and mustard
Mashed avocado, a little lemon juice and garlic.
Smoked salmon bits or pate and chopped dill.
Mashed pâté
Don't prepare to long before serving as they do go soft. This is why it is important to dry the pastry out well.

To Cook:
Aga in the roasting oven for 15-20 minutes. Remove from the oven, make a hole to release the steam and then put them in the simmering oven to dry out about 15 minutes.
Electric fan oven 180ºC (Gas Mark 7) for 20-25 minutes).
Remove from the oven, make a hole to release the steam and reduce the temperature to 130ºC (Gas Mark 1) for a further 20 minutes.
Allow to cool and fill.

Gougere of Fish, Game or Vegatables

Make up the choux paste as normal, but at the end of the beating add 60g of diced or grated cheese, salt, pepper and 1tsp mustard. Butter a 25cm ovenproof dish and spread the choux pastry around the edges of the dish with a very thin layer in the middle.

Fillings:

Game or Ham
This is a great way to use up just 100g of left over game or ham., Add a few mushrooms, onion, some herbs and a dash of Worcestershire sauce to make a tasty sauce, made with stock or milk.

Spread the sauce in the centre of the dish and cook.

Fish:

Make an onion and tomato sauce, or a cheese sauce. Add 100g - 200g cooked fish: cod, smoked haddock, salmon or prawns and lots of herbs.

Vegetables:
Sauté some onion and garlic. Add curry powder or rogan josh seasoning and 1tbs of flour. Stir this and add a selection of fresh vegetables and 150ml stock. Place in the choux and cook

To Cook:

Aga: Cook in the roasting oven on the grid shelf on the bottom set of runners for 30-45 minutes until well risen and crispy.

Electric fan oven at 180°c (Gas mark 7) for 45 minutes

Cheese Pastry Bats and Things

This is a pastry recipe that is useful for little savouries. I am always buying cutters when I see them and at the party shop in Oxford I found a great little set of Halloween cutters - bats, ghosts, cats and pumpkins. They are ideal for the Halloween dip! This recipe is very rich. If the children want to make biscuits, you can also use the cheese pastry recipe from June - that is easier to handle.

Ingredients:

115g Plain flour
115g Hard cold butter
90g Tasty cheese, Cheddar,
Double Gloucester if you want a
more colourful pastry, or Parmesan,
grated very finely
1 tbs Cold water
2 tsp mustard powder
1/4 tsp cayenne pepper
Salt

Method:

1. Sift the flour into a bowl with the mustard powder, cayenne and a good pinch of salt.

2. Grate the butter. Add the butter and cheese to the flour and mix together with a round bladed knife.

3. Add the cold water. Mix to a firm, but not stiff, dough. Knead gently until smooth and refrigerate for 1/2 an hour.

4. Roll out and cut into shapes or straws for dipping. Cook on a lined baking tray until firm.

5. Allow to cool on a cooling rack. They will keep in an airtight tin - make sure they are really cold before boxing.

This pastry can be cut into small rounds or squares as bases for little savouries.

Aga on the grid shelf on the floor of the roasting oven for about 5 - 7 minutes.

Electric fan oven at 170°C (Gas mark 7) for 5 - 7 minutes.

Bramble Suet Pudding

Time for a good old fashioned suet pud. It's cold enough in October! These are such good value and can be made quickly. Once made they are happy to stay in the oven until required. I've given you a bramble pudding but you can use 450g of whatever fruit is available.

Ingredients:

Suet crust pastry:
170g Plain flour
60 g Fresh breadcrumbs
1 tsp Baking powder
20g Sugar
Pinch of salt
130g Suet
150ml Water or milk
or a mixture of both
FILLING:
450g -500g Fruit, 300g Blackberries
and 200g Peeled and Chopped
Apples
100 g Soft brown sugar
2 tbs Water
40g Butter
Butter for greasing the bowl

Method:

1. Fill a large saucepan with 6-8 cms. water and bring it to the boil.

2. In a bowl mix together the dry ingredients, add the cold water and cut together with a round bladed knife to form a soft but not sticky dough, roll 2/3 of the pastry into a circle1-2 cms. thick.

3. Grease the cooking bowl really well with butter and line the bowl with the circle of pastry, add the prepared fruit mixed with the sugar add 2 tbs. water and dot over the 40 gms of butter.

4. Roll out the rest of the pastry, wet the top edge of the pastry put on the top and seal the edges. Put the lid on the bowl or a piece of double foil with a pleat across the top, crimp the foil over the rim of the bowl to form a lid and lower into the saucepan of boiling water and cook:

Aga: Put the saucepan on the floor of the roasting oven for 30 mins. then move to the simmering oven for another 3 hours or so!

Electric or Gas: Simmer gently for 3-4 hours on the hob, check and top up the water when necessary.

To serve, remove carefully from the saucepan, take off the lid, run a knife around the pud and turn it out, good old fashioned custard is perfect with this, even Birds with 3-4 tbs. double cream stirred through will do!

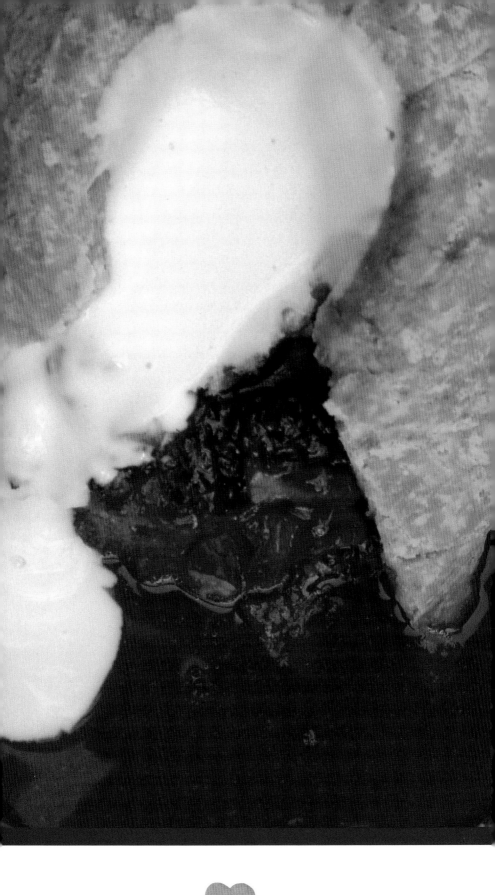

Coxes and Calvados

Ingredients:

750g Cox's apples
250g Granulated sugar
60ml Water
10cm Cinnamon stick
5 Cloves
Zest and juice of a lemon
100ml. Calvados
To serve: Whipped cream, lemon zest and mint leaves

Method:

1. Put the water, sugar, cinnamon, cloves and lemon in a saucepan. Bring to the boil and simmer for 5 minutes (if you like a delicate flavour remove the cinnamon and cloves now.)

2. Peel and core the apples but keep them whole. Drop them into the syrup.

3. Bring the syrup to the boil and then poach the apples until tender on very low heat. This will take 30 - 45 minutes. This is done on the hob or in the simmering oven of the **Aga**.

4. Once cooked, remove from the heat. Add the Calvados and allow the apples to cool in the syrup.

5. Carefully lift the apples out and serve with whipped cream in the centre hole with a twist of lemon zest and a mint leaf.

Totally Nutty Treacle Bread and Butter Pud

I've just made this recipe up as I hadn't got a bread and butter pudding for October. I hope it works - I'll try it tomorrow!

Ingredients:

1 Small fruit loaf, sliced and buttered
100g Brazil nuts
100g Walnuts
2 tbs Black treacle
300ml Milk
2 Eggs

Method:

1. Put the black treacle in a bowl. Warm it on the back of the Aga or in the microwave for 1 min. at 360 watt so that the treacle becomes runny.

2. Butter an ovenproof dish and the fruit bread. Cut the slices in half and line the dish.

3. Roughly chop the nuts and put a generous layer over the bread. Add another layer of bread and then the remaining nuts.

4. Add the milk and eggs to the treacle. Mix them together and pour them into the dish. Allow the pudding to stand for 30 minutes before cooking.

Aga: Cook on the grid shelf on the floor of the roasting oven for 20-30 minutes

Electric fan oven at 170°c (Gas mark 6) for 20-30 minutes
Cook in a combination oven at 180°c with 360 watt microwave or 15-20 minutes

Jane:-
Tomorrow, I tried it, it is still here, it was pretty good, very nutty, give it a try!

Auntie Nan's ginger biscuits

These are the best dunking biscuits in the world. I love visiting Auntie Nan, not only to catch up on all her news, but also in the certainty that there will be ginger biscuits. Mine never seem to dunk quite as well as the ones she makes!

Ingredients:

110g Margarine or Butter
80g Castor Sugar
1tbs Golden Syrup
170g Self Raising Flour
1/2 tsp Bicarbonate of Soda
1 tsp Ground Ginger (add a little more if you like a really gingery flavour I use 2 tsp)

Method:

1. Melt together the butter, sugar and syrup.

2. Sift the dry ingredients into the mixture. Beat it all together.

3. Place small teaspoonfuls on a lined baking tray and bake.

4. This mixture can be rolled into sausages and shaped into gingerbread men, remember it spreads a lot, and then decorate with water icing, eyes and buttons etc!

Aga: Cook in the roasting oven for approximately 10 minutes on the grid shelf on the floor of the oven. Alternatively cook more slowly in the baking oven for about 20 minutes on the bottom set of runners.

Electric fan oven at 160°c
Gas mark 5) for 10-15 minutes.

Excellent Christmas Cake

I know it isn't Christmas ,but it is time to make the cake! This is my nut-less recipe that seems very popular, especially at Bell's my local Aga distributor. At Bell's they've been eating it for years and keep asking for more of the same, all year round! With this and my baked ham (which comes in December) Keith, John, Steve, Bernie and Tim are happy bunnies!! They look after me well too!

Ingredients:

400g Sultanas
500g Raisins
125g Currants
150g Glace Cherries
150g Mixed Peel
150ml Brandy or Sherry
225g Butter
225g Soft brown sugar
1tsp Orange Rind - grated
1tsp Lemon Rind - grated
1/8tsp Almond Essence
1tsp Vanilla Essence
2tbs Marmalade
1tsp Black Treacle
4 Eggs
350g Plain Flour
Pinch of Salt
1tsp Mixed Spice
1/4tsp Ground Cinnamon
1/4tsp Nutmeg

Method:

1. Wash and dry the fruit and place in a large bowl. Pour over the brandy and mix well. Cover and leave to stand overnight.

2. Prepare an 20-24cm round cake tin: Line with bake-o-glide and put a double thickness of brown paper around the outside of the tin (or newspaper).

3. Cream the butter and sugar together until light and fluffy. Add fruit rinds, essences and marmalade. Beat well.

4. Add the eggs one at a time, beating well after each addition. If the mixture starts to curdle, add a little of the flour.

5. Fold in the prepared fruits, alternating them with the dry ingredients. Mix well.

6. Pour into a lined tin. Smooth over the top and bake.

Aga in the simmering oven for
5-12 hours until cooked

Electric fan oven at 140°C
(Gas mark 2) for 3-4 hours

This can be cooked on combination
at 130°c fan oven with180 Watts
microwave for the first 30 minutes
and 90 Watts for the last 30 minutes.

The cake is ready when a skewer
inserted in the centre comes out
clean. Let the cake cool in the
tin, and then take it out and wrap
up until it's time to decorate it for
Christmas.
(It can be spiked with a little more
brandy).

Trick or Treat Treacle Toffee

This recipe appears by kind permission of my sister Mary. This is a great seller at the Harvest sales!

Ingredients:

220g Butter
220g Black treacle
330g Demerara sugar
100ml Water
1 tsp Mustard powder
Pinch of cream of tartar

Method:

1. In a really large saucepan melt together the butter, treacle, sugar, mustard powder and water.

2. When it comes to the boil add the cream of tartar. Keep stirring the mixture as it boils for about 20 minutes until setting point is reached.

3. Setting point is reached when a drop of the mixture forms a ball when dropped in cold water. If you have a sugar thermometer it's at 120°c-122°c.

4. Once setting point is reached, pour the mixture into a lined shallow baking tray or well buttered tin.

5. Allow the mixture to go cold. Take it out of the tin and break it up with a hammer!

6. This makes 7 x 125g bags of toffee. Lots of Treats for you to enjoy!

November

American Thanksgiving is on the last Thursday of November, so we've got American influences. I'm not doing the turkey though - check in your oven instruction book for cooking times for that - but I've put in some ideas for stuffing and beyond! November also brings my son's birthday, so his favourite pudding is in here. It is also bonfire night, although this overlaps with Halloween ideas. I have lots of walnuts off my tree in November, dried and ready to cook or eat, and excellent with creamy Stilton and a glass of Elderberry Port!

RECIPES

Creamy Fish Soup

Peanut Bread

Potted Pork

Squash Chilli and Walnuts

Stuffing News

Vegetable Strudel

Couscous

Pumpkin Pasta

Beef Chicago

Williams Potatoes

Sri Lankan Chicken Cadjugama

Cranberry, Cheese and Onion Bread and Butter Pudding

Swiss Roll

Baked Alaska

Pecan and Pumpkin Pie

Kay's Kookies

Creamy Fish Soup

This soup came about after a dear friend Chuff (who enjoys food as much as I do!), returned from visiting her daughter in Helsinki. She waxed lyrical about this wonderful fish soup she had eaten there, and so I set about to create it. I'm not sure if this is like the one Chuff had, but I liked it enough to want to share it with you!

Ingredients:

1 Large undyed smoked haddock fillet, not essential to be undyed but it makes it pale and interesting!
1 Dry smoked salmon fillet
1 Fresh salmon fillet
3-4 Sprigs dill
2 Bay leaves
3 Blades mace
6 Peppercorns
Milk to cover
50 g Flour
150 ml Cream
20g Dill, chopped

Method:

1. Place all the fish skin side up in an ovenproof dish with the seasonings and cover with milk.

2. To Cook
   Aga on the grid shelf in the roasting oven for 15-20 mins.
   Electric fan oven 160°c (Gas mark 5) for 20 mins.
   Allow the fish to cool in the milk.

3. Take the haddock out of the milk and liquidize until smooth, keep the salmon whole and refrigerate until serving the soup.
   Strain the milk.

4. Make a white sauce with the butter, flour and milk, if it needs more liquid add some water and then the pureed fish, adjust the seasoning and reheat, add half of the dill and stir in the cream reheat but don't boil it!

5. Pour into warm soup bowls and break up a few bits of the salmon in the centre of each bowl of soup and sprinkle with more chopped dill.
   Wedges of peanut bread can be served with this soup.

Peanut Bread

Ingredients:

340 g Plain flour
1/2 tsp Salt
1/2 tsp Cream of tartar
1/2 tsp bicarbonate of soda
30g Chopped salted peanuts
30g Whole salted peanuts
200ml Milk
2 tbs Chopped dill

Method:

1. Mix together the dry ingredients in a bowl.

2. Add the milk. Bind the mixture together with a round bladed knife.
    Knead it very lightly and shape into a round about 3cm thick. Cut it into 8 wedges, keeping it in the round. Place it on a lined baking tray and cook

3. **Aga** on the floor of the roasting oven for 15 minutes
    Electric fan oven at 180°c (Gas mark7) for 20 minutes

4   Serve buttered with soup, such as the fish soup. The bread is best eaten immediately, it doesn't keep!

Different herbs can be used.
Olives or sun dried tomatoes can be added instead of the peanuts.

261

Potted Pork

A simple potted meat the long slow cooking just melts away the fat and gives wonderfully tender meat, a starter, a lunch , a snack!

Ingredients:

1¹/2 kg Belly pork, boned and the skin scored
Salt
2 Cloves garlic, crushed
2 Bay leaves
A few sprigs of parsley, sage and thyme
6-8 Peppercorns

Method:

1. Rub the pork all over with salt and leave in a cool place overnight.

2. Cut the meat into strips 4-5 cm. wide and place in an enamel roasting tin, with the herbs, garlic and peppercorns and 100ml water.

3. Start the cooking in a really hot oven for 30 minutes and then reduce the temperature and cook for at least 4 hours. The meat should be soft and swimming in fat, don't mention the cholesterol!

4. Check seasoning. Remove any crackling.

5. Strain the fat through a sieve. Put the strained fat to one side and keep.   Shred the meat by pulling it apart with a pair of forks.

6. Loosely fill little earthenware pots with the meat. Pour the fat over the meat and let it set in the refrigerator

Always serve at room temperature, with toast and a good marmalade or chutney e.g. Apricot (in July)or Chutneys (September) and gerkins! I just love the crunchy texture of gerkins with the soft pork.

Aga hanging on the top set of runners in the roasting oven for 30 minutes. Then move to the simmering oven and cook for at least 4 hours until really tender.

Electric fan oven at 180°c (Gas mark 7) for 30 minutes
Then reduce to 130°c (Gas mark1) for at least 4 hours

Squash Chilli and Walnuts

America meets England in this recipe. Looking at my tree this 2001 is a bumper year for walnuts. The contrast of the crunchy nuts with the soft chunks of squash, enhanced by chilli flakes, garlic and herbs, is good for either Thanksgiving or Christmas.

Ingredients:

500g Squash
3 tbs Oil
2 Cloves garlic
1/4 tsp Chilli flakes
50g Walnuts
Salt and pepper
1 tbs Chopped parsley

Method:

1. Peel and de-seed the squash. Cut into even sizes and place in a bowl. Add the oil, chopped cloves of garlic, chilli flakes, roughly chopped walnuts, salt and pepper.

2. Toss it all together. Place in a roasting tin and cook.

Aga in the roasting oven for 20-30 minutes

Electric fan oven at 170°c (Gas mark 6) for 20-30- minutes depending on the size of the squash.

3. Put in the serving dish and scatter the chopped parsley over it.

For a speedy supper this mixture can be mixed with leftover turkey or fish (or even a tin of tuna or salmon). Sprinkle the mixture liberally with a well flavoured cheese and bake for just 10-15 minutes in a hot oven.

Stuffing News

Plan ahead for Christmas or have a trial run on Thanksgiving Day, the last Thursday in November! These are ideas to serve with the turkey, other poultry or any meat. Most of the stuffings below are suitable for vegetarians.   Some do have bacon or panchetta, but this can be left out.

Poultry

The ruling now about stuffing is NOT to put it in the cavity of the bird.
A little stuffing can go in the neck end, a pork forcemeat which is made with sausagemeat is good. This will add fat to the bird as well.

Pork

A nice boned shoulder or leg of pork can be stuffed - it's delicious at this time of the year.
Remember though, when you have stuffed the pork joint, weigh it again to get the total weight for the cooking time. Stuffing can be fairly solid so needs to be included for the cooking time.

Onions

To stuff onions I normally throw the onions in their skins in the oven for 30 minutes first.
Then cut the onions in half across the rings. Remove the centres and add them chopped to the stuffing mix, and pile the stuffing in the cavity.

Other Vegetables

Other vegetables can usually be stuffed raw.
If you are stuffing tomatoes cut the tops off or cut them in half, depending on the size. Sprinkle a little salt inside and turn them upside down to drain to remove some of the moisture.
If you want to stuff cabbage leaves, choose unblemished leaves.
To make the cabbage leaves more pliable blanche them in boiling salted water for 2 minutes. Then cool immediately.
Roll the stuffing up inside the leaf, put in a greased dish and then pour a tomato sauce around, or a tin of the tomato and herbs and cook.
Marrow can be simmered for a few minutes before stuffing too.
A little stock or sauce poured around the vegetables gives instant sauce, but is not essential.

To cook stuffed vegetables :

Aga in the roasting oven for 20-40 minutes depending on the size
of the vegetables and the type of stuffing.

Electric fan oven at 170°c for 20-40 minutes
Cook in a combination oven at 170°c
with 600 watt microwave for10-15 minutes

Stuffing News

Pork Forcemeat

There are lots of interesting sausages on the market - I always fancied running a shop that just sold sausages!

Ingredients

Sausages or sausagemeat, Onions, mushrooms, celery, herbs, cooked chestnuts (optional) and Breadcrumbs

Method:

1. Select a sausage containing a combination of flavours that you like.

   Take the sausages out of their skins to use them for the forcemeat. You can add extras if you wish!

   Alternatively you can add the following to plain sausagemeat:
   a sauteed onion, some mushrooms, some finely chopped celery and lots of chopped herbs.

   Add 50g of breadcrumbs to each 400g of sausagemeat.
   Roasted chopped chestnuts or other nuts can also be added.

   Once you have made up the forcemeat, stuff it into the neck end of the turkey. Pull the flap of skin well over to hold it in.

   Add the weight of the stuffing to the weight of the turkey
   for the cooking time.

   For cooking times of the turkey or other meat, refer to the instruction book of your oven!

My Perennial Stuffing

Each time I make this it is always different! I sauté the ingredients gently in a roasting tin in the roasting oven or cook them in the microwave on 600watts, with some dripping, or butter and oil.

Ingredients:

Onion, chopped
Bacon or panchetta
Celery, sliced
Cranberries or raisins, big fat juicy Lexia ones or ready to eat dried apricots, chopped.
Walnuts or chestnuts chopped
A splash of wine or brandy
Lots of chopped parsley
A little chopped thyme
Zest and juice of an orange, lemon or lime
Spices if you like e.g. nutmeg, chilli flakes
Breadcrumbs
Salt and Pepper
Egg

Method:

1. Mix the onion, bacon and celery together and sauté.

2. Add the cranberries, walnuts, wine, citrus juice and herbs.

3. Add enough breadcrumbs to start to hold it together. Then add lots of salt and pepper.

4. Beat the egg and add it to the mixture. (I don't always add this.)

5. Place the stuffing in a well greased dish. Dot with butter and cook for about 30 minutes in the oven with the meat or poultry until slightly crispy on the top.

6. Cut into squares, triangles or diamonds and serve with the bird!

7. If you have added the egg, the stuffing can be rolled into balls and the baked in a greased dish until browned and crisp. You could also deep fat fry them.

Vegetarian Strudel or Pie

Omit the bacon or panchetta (some grated cheese could be added).

1. Spread the stuffing onto 4 layers of buttered filo pastry.

2. Roll it up like a strudel and cook in a hot oven for 20-30 minutes.

3. Serve as nibbles in thin slices. Alternatively for supper cut it into wedges and serve with a mixed salad.

To make a pie:
Put it on a baking tray between a top and bottom of puff pastry.

1. Seal the edges well with beaten egg wash. Brush egg wash over the top as well.

2. Cook in a hot oven again for 20-30 minutes until the pastry is cooked and golden brown. This is good served with a tomato or cheesy sauce.

Other additions to Breadcrumbs for stuffing

Mushrooms, onion, garlic, bacon and herbs

Chopped apple, cut up ready to eat prunes, chopped cashew nuts, lemon zest and juice and herbs

Assorted chopped nuts (walnuts, brazil nuts, cashews), onion, mushrooms and herbs.

Ready to eat Apricots, with mixed spice, lemon juice. Mint or rosemary are my favourite herbs with this. I also add 1-2 tbs suet to the breadcrumbs as well if it is a lean joint and needs some fat . If you are sauteing any of the ingredients then you do not need to add the suet.

Couscous

Couscous can be used as an alterative to the breadcrumbs.

Soak the couscous in double its volume of hot water or stock. Leave it to absorb the water.

Add your choice of the following:

Dried fruits go well:
> Apricots, prunes, cranberries, raisins, and sultanas
> Zest and juice of citrus fruits
> Chopped onion, garlic, tomatoes, peeled peppers,
> nuts, grated fresh root ginger
> A little ground cinnamon, allspice
> or coriander seeds and chopped fresh coriander too
> Some chopped Chorizo, other sausage, cured ham or bacon

If you are using the mixture to stuff vegetables, you can use the last option to make a more substantial meal.

For a vegetarian option you can substitute grated vegetarian cheese for the meat.

The choice is yours of what you add to your base ingredients to the stuffing, just create your own from the lists above or from what you have in your store cupboard or the refrigerator.

Pumpkin Pasta

The pumpkin is here - another Thanksgiving recipe! There is also pumpkin about to be dealt with after Halloween and this is one way to do that, using the pumpkin to make a sauce to go with pasta.

Pasta needs to be cooked in fast boiling water and according to the time on the packet. I haven't succumbed to making my own pasta yet, but I believe it dries well on the front rail of the Aga!

Ingredients:

500g Fresh pasta or 300 g Dried pasta
500g Peeled pumpkin
1 Large onion chopped
3 Bay leaves
A Blade of mace or 1/4 tsp grated nutmeg
Salt and pepper
1 Red pepper deseeded, skinned and chopped
OR 100-150 g Cooked meat or salami
4-6 tbs Soured cream or crÉme fraiche
50 g Pumpkin seeds
1 tbs Oil
Fresh herbs to garnish

Method:

1. Put the oil in a saucepan with the pumpkin seeds. Cook until the seeds are golden. Remove the seeds from the pan and keep them warm.

2. Roughly chop the pumpkin flesh and the onion.

3. Place them in the pan with the bay leaves and mace or nutmeg and some seasoning. Add 100ml water and simmer until tender. (Do this in the Aga simmering oven.)

4. Remove the bay leaves and mace . Beat or mash the pumpkin. Beat in the soured cream and season.

5. Cook the pasta according to the instructions.

6. Chop up the cooked meat or
   salami. Add this to the sauce. If
   you are using the pepper add
   this to the sauce instead of the
   meat for a vegetarian version.

7. Pour the sauce over the pasta.
   Scatter the pumpkin seeds
   and chopped fresh herbs over
   the top.

   Grated or diced cheese can be
   served with this. A salad also
   goes nicely.

Beef Chicago

This recipe came into being when I was demonstrating in Chicago. What a great, fun city Chicago is. It's the cattle yard of America and is a hot and exciting place, so for Chicago I put a red hot paste around wonderful fillet of beef. This recipe is a good alternative for Thanksgiving. My son's birthday is 23rd November and it has become a favourite for his birthday too. Meat cooked en croûte is always good for special occasions as it can be prepared for the oven beforehand and then popped in the oven at just the right time.No matter how delayed your guests are!

Ingredients:

2 Red peppers (chopped)
1 Onion (chopped)
3 tbs Sun dried tomato puree
2 Cloves garlic (chopped)
Chilli flakes can be added, some like it hot!
2 tsp Whole grain mustard
2 tbs Chopped parsley
1 tbs Chopped oregano
2 pkts Ready made puff pastry
Butter and olive oil
Black pepper and dry mustard
800g-1kg Fillet steak (approx. 100g per person)
1 Egg mixed with milk to make egg wash to glaze pastry

Method:

1. Place the fillet, well seasoned, in the roasting tin on the floor of roasting oven, in an electric fan oven at 180°c (Gas mark 7) or in a frying pan.

2. Seal the meat very quickly for 20 mins to seal in juices, turning it half way through cooking.

3. Remove the meat and allow it to go cold.

4. Sauté the onions, peppers and garlic until well softened and reducied to a nice thick paste. Add the tomato puree, herbs and seasoning, let this go cold.

5. Roll out the pastry into two neat oblong 6-8 cm larger than the piece of meat.

6. Spread half of tomato mixture onto the pastry where the meat will sit.

7. Place the beef on top of the tomato mixture and cover it with remainder of tomato mixture. Place the other piece of pastry on top and pinch the edges together to seal and brush over with egg wash.

8. Decorate (write beef in left over pastry or make leaves!)

9. Brush the Beef Chicago well with egg wash. Place it on a bake-o-glide lined baking tray and cook.

10. You can cook the dish for longer than the time specified if you want the beef 'well done.'

11. Serve Beef Chicago with simple vegetables and Williams potatoes (the recipe follows).

Cook the Beef Chicago from room temperature, if cooked straight from the refrigerator it will take longer to cook

Aga: Place on the floor of the roasting oven for 15 mins, before moving higher up in the oven for additional 15 mins to brown. Total cooking time should be 30 minutes,for rare, 40 minutes for medium and 50 -60 minutes for well done

Electric fan oven at 180°c (Gas mark 7)

Williams Potatoes

These weren't named after me! They were actually named after the pear. They are simply croquette potatoes, shaped into a pear shape! Again these can be prepared in advance and simply popped in the oven to cook.

Ingredients:

500g Freshly boiled potatoes
2 Egg yolks
30g Butter
A little hot milk
Salt and pepper
Breadcrumbs, fresh or dried
2 tbs Ground almonds
1 Eegg
A stalk of spaghetti
Some whole cloves

Method:

1. Boil the potatoes until soft. Mash them well.

2. Add the egg yolks, butter, seasoning and enough milk to make a smooth but not too soft mixture. Beat until smooth.

3. Divide the mashed potato into pear size portions on a floured board. Allow the potato to go cold.

4. Shape the potato into a pear shape. Brush it with beaten egg and then toss it in a mixture of breadcrumbs and ground almonds mixed together.

5. Place a small piece of spaghetti in the top to form the stalk and a clove for the eye of the pear.

6. Put on a lined baking tray and bake.

7. These can be deep fat fried, but I prefer to keep the fat content down and cook them in the oven!

To cook:

Aga in the roasting oven for 20-30 minutes depending on the size of the "pears".
Alternatively cook in the top of the baking oven for 30 minutes

Electric fan oven at 170°c (Gas mark 6) for 20-30 minutes

Sri Lankan Chicken Cadjugama

I bought this recipe home from a holiday in Sri Lanka. Sri Lanka is a beautiful country full of lovely people and coconut palms! This was a recipe that the hotel chef shared with us, I hope you like it too. The recipe uses the delicious cashew nuts that they grow in Sri Lanka, where they are sold by beautiful ladies at the side of the road!

Ingredients:

400g Boned chicken meat in large chunks
100g Cashew nuts
2 tbs Oil
75g Chopped onion
3 Cloves garlic
1 tsp Turmeric
1 tsp Grated fresh ginger
1/2 Small stalk lemon grass
1 tbs Curry leaves
A pinch of saffron strands
2 tsp Curry powder
1/2 tsp Chilli powder
10 cm Cinnamon stick
4 Cardamon seeds
3-4 Whole cloves
50 g Tomatoes, skinned and seeded
100ml Coconut milk

Method:

1. Put the cashew nuts in a saucepan and just cover them with water. Add the turmeric and simmer for 30 minutes.

2. Allow to cool slightly before draining. The water can then be used to cook the rice in.

3. Heat the oil in a frying or sauté pan. Add the onion, garlic, curry and chilli powder. Let them start to cook and then add the chicken and all the other spices.

4. Seal the chicken and then add the tomatoes and the coconut milk. Cook very gently until tender (it should take about 8 minutes). Stir it regularly to prevent the coconut milk curdling.

5. Once the chicken is cooked, remove the cinnamon stick, the cloves and lemon grass.

6. Stir in the cashew nuts and heat them through.

7. Serve with rice and a salad.

Cranberry, Cheese and Onion Bread and Butter Pudding

A savoury bread and butter pudding this month. Cranberries have a sharp acidic taste that goes well with cheese. You could use a blue cheese - Stilton is at its best at this time of the year, although it is perhaps an acquired taste in this dish. I like to crumble the cheese into this dish so a tasty Lancashire or Cheshire is good. Fresh or pickled onions can be used!

Ingredients:

8-12 Rounds of bread and butter
200g Cheese, crumbled or grated
100g Onion
100g Fresh cranberries
2 Eggs
300 ml Creamy milk
6 Sage leaves, chopped
Salt, pepper and a little grated nutmeg if you like it

Method:

1. Butter an ovenproof dish. Line with a layer of bread and butter.

2. Scatter some of the cheese, onion, cranberries and sage over the bread. Add another layer of bread and butter. Put the rest of the cheese, onion, cranberries and the sage on top.

3. Beat together the eggs and the milk. Season and pour over the mixture.

4. Allow to stand for at least 15 minutes before baking.

5. Bake until crisp and golden brown. Serve with a crisp green salad.

To bake:

Aga on the grid shelf on the floor of
the roasting oven for 20-30 minutes

Electric fan oven170°c
(Gas mark 6) for 20-30 minutes
Cook in a combination oven at
180°c with 360 watt microwave for
12- 20 minutes

Swiss Roll

Ingredients:

4 eggs
110g Caster Sugar
110g Plain Flour
400g Jam

Method:

1. Whisk together the sugar and eggs until thick and creamy.

2. Fold in the flour and place in lined tin, bake.

3. **Aga** bottom set of runners in the roasting oven for 6 minutes.

   Electric fan oven 170°C (Gas Mark 6) for 10-15 minutes.

   Remove from oven and allow to cool slightly .

5. Roll up - see pictures.

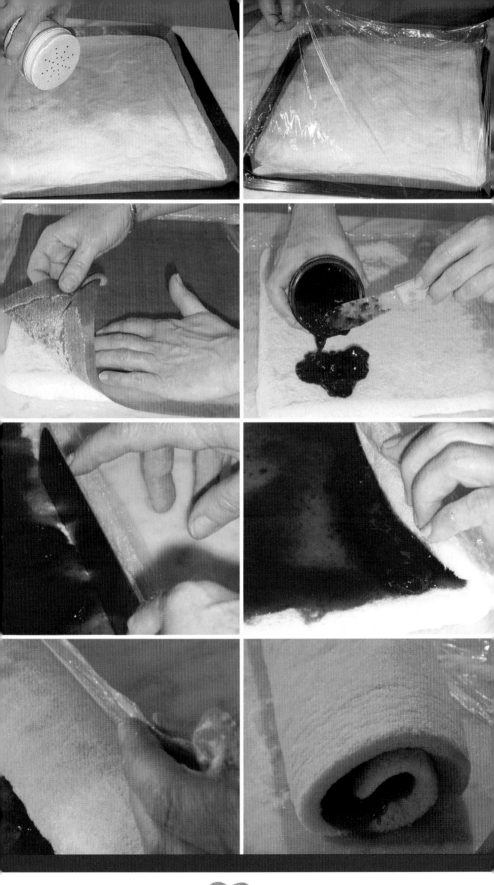

Baked Alaska

I have baked for this Tom's birthday every year since he could talk and decide what he would like. It has definitely stood the test of time, as he is now 23! If you are in a hurry you can use shop-bought Swiss roll and tinned strawberries. If you have time you can make a quick 3 or 4 egg Swiss roll and use fresh strawberries. The strawberries are lovely sliced and marinated with grated ginger and a tbs of castor sugar. An alternative is sugar and 2 tbs of balsamic vinegar or a fruit vinegar, or zest and juice of an orange.

Ingredients:

1 Swiss roll
Strawberries or your favourite soft fruit
2 tsp Grated fresh root ginger and 1tbs Castor sugar
A block of ice cream
5 egg whites
300g Caster sugar

Method:

1. Slice the strawberries. Add the ginger and the 1tbs sugar. Leave to marinate.

2. Cut the Swiss roll into slices and arrange in an ovenproof dish. Sprinkle over some of the juice from the strawberries.

3. Beat the egg whites until really thick and glossy. Beat in a third of the sugar, beat again, add another third, beat and then fold in the final third.

4. Place the ice cream on the sponge cake. Cover with the strawberries and finally the meringue. Make sure that the meringue seals in all the other ingredients.

5. Bake

6. Serve straight away and Enjoy!

Aga for 5 minutes in the roasting oven on the bottom set of runners.

Electric fan oven 180°c
(Gas mark 7) for 5 minutes precisely

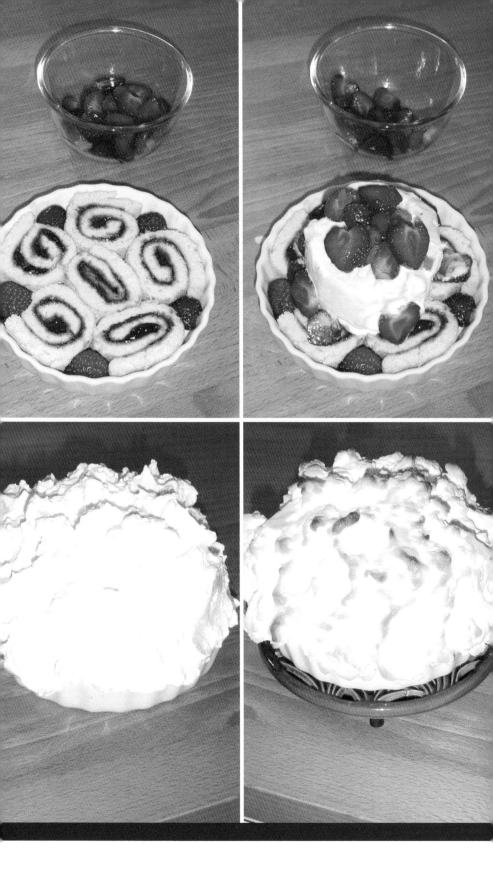

Pecan and Pumpkin Pie

I am not a fan of Pumpkin Pie but it does go with Thanksgiving. I find this recipe has an interesting texture and hides the pumpkin in the Pecan Pie!

Ingredients:

350g Sweet short crust pastry
150g Pumpkin cooked and mashed
3eggs
120g Syrup - Maple or golden
200g Pecan nuts, chopped
A few drops vanilla essences

Topping:

70g soft brown sugar
150g pecan nuts
3tbs honey or syrup
50g. Butter

Method:

1. Line 25cm flan tin with the pastry

2. Whisk together the eggs, vanilla essence and syrup. Add the mashed pumpkin,and nuts.

3. Pour the mixture into the flan case. Bake until the edges are browned.

Aga on the floor of the roasting oven for 20-35 minutes

Electric fan oven at 170°c (Gas mark 6) for about 30 minutes until firm to the touch
If your oven has a bottom heat function use this set at 200°c for about 25-30 minutes

4. While the pie is cooking, melt the topping ingredients together on the back of the Aga or in the microwave at 360watt for 3 mins.

5. Remove the pie from the oven and leave to rest and firm up before spooning the topping over the pie.

6. Serve - it's delicious served with Greek yogurt.

Kay's Kookies

The first demonstration I gave at home was to a delightful group of American Aga owners. Kay and her husband, Bernard, were part of that group. Kay very kindly shared this recipe with me and I would like to share it with you as a tin of these goes well beside the bonfire! Other ideas for eating by the bonfire can be picked up from October and Halloween!

Ingredients:

160g Butter
150g Caster sugar
2tsp Black treacle
1 Egg
85g Self raising flour
85g Plain flour
60g Whole meal flour
1 tsp Ground ginger
1 tsp Ground cinnamon
1/4 tsp Ground cloves
1/4 tsp Ground nutmeg
1 tsp Bicarbonate of soda
1/2 tsp Salt

Method:

1. Melt together the butter, sugar and treacle. Allow to cool.

2. Sift together the dry ingredients. Add the egg and the cooled butter mix. Beat well and then chill for one hour.

3. Place teaspoonfuls of the mixture on a lined baking sheet and bake.

Aga on the grid shelf on the floor of the baking oven for 8-10 minutes depending on whether you want a chewy middle!

Electric fan oven at 160°c (Gas mark 5) for 8-10 minutes

December

I wish you a Merry Christmas and a Happy New Year! My present to you is some of the simple alternatives to the traditional which you have asked me for again and again. There are two of my Mum's recipes that go on forever. These recipes always tug on so many happy memories each time I cook them - what a delicious way to be remembered! I almost got into trouble with my vegetarian friend for not including enough vegetarian recipes in this chapter, but for a vegetarian dish the turkey can be removed from the Turkey cakes, and lots of roasted nuts stirred into the red cabbage takes that to another dimension!

RECIPES

Roast Goose

Gravy

Prawn and Apple Starter

Plum Sauce with Gin

Plum Chutney

Cranberry Mash

Sprouts Go Nuts

Red Cabbage

Christmas Gammon

Turkey Cakes

Cranberry Salsa

Mustard Mayo

Mincemeat Bread and Bread Pudding

Auntie Mary's Christmas Pud

Figs with Mascarpone

Chocolate Almond Log

Mincemeat Stars

Sarah's Truffles

Hazelnut Clusters

Almond Fancies

Peppermint Creams

Roast Goose

This is the traditional seasonal bird for the Christmas table. Goose always provides an enjoyable alternative to the turkey. There was an old wives tale that it is good luck to eat goose at Michaelmas - 21st September. This was called a green goose as it had fed on green grass as opposed to the Christmas bird which is fattened on the stubble of the corn fields! Do remember that you need about 600g of goose per person as it is always very fatty. The fat should always be kept - not for rubbing the chest as a cough and cold remedy - but to cook the best ever roast potatoes in as it has a high burning point!

Juniper is a good flavour to go with the goose. Goose needs a sharp acid contrast, such as plums, spiked with a slug of gin!

Ingredients:

4-5 kg Oven ready goose
1 Small onion
2-3 Plums
Cloves of garlic (if you like garlic!)
A few sage leaves
Salt
Flour

Method:

1. Wipe out the goose and trim any excessive fat. Keep the fat and melt it down to use for cooking.

2. Roughly cut up the onion and the plums. Place the onion, plums, sage and garlic (optional) in the cavity of the bird.

3. Prick the skin well. Rub the skin with salt and dust it with flour.

4. Place the bird on a grill rack in the roasting tin, breast side down and roast.

Aga

Cook in the roasting oven for 30 minutes.

Turn the goose over and brown the breast for a further 30 minutes.

Place the goose in the simmering oven for a further hour at least.

Return the goose to the roasting oven to crisp the skin for 30 minutes

Allow to rest for 30 minutes before carving.

The goose will not come to any harm left in the simmering oven for longer.

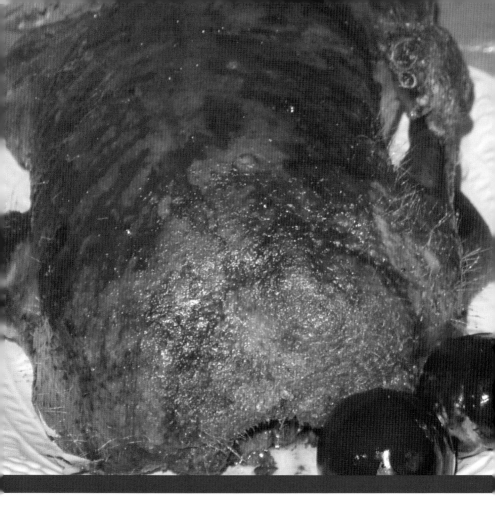

Electric fan oven at 170°c (Gas mark 6) for 45 minutes

Reduce the temperature to 160°c (Gas mark 4) for the remainder of the cooking
time 2-2¹/₂hours total cooking time,

You can increase the temperature to 180°c (Gas mark 6) for the last 35 minutes to crisp up the skin if necessary.

The goose is cooked when the juices run clear when a skewer it pushed through the thigh joint and the breast.

If the goose is very fatty pour the excess fat out of the roasting tin during the cooking and use this to roast the potatoes in!

The Gravy

The best gravy is made using the giblets. You can remove the liver and make pate with this - use the chicken liver pate recipe from April with additional chicken livers to make up the quantities. This gives a really rich pâté which makes an easy canape, just spread on some toast.

Ingredients:

The giblets
Onion, stuck with 3 cloves
3 Bay leaves
2 Sprigs of sage
2 Sticks celery
1 Carrot, cut up
Flour
A little wine

Method:

1. Place all the giblets in a saucepan and add the onion, bay leaves, herbs, celery, carrot, salt and pepper.

2. Cover with water and bring slowly to the boil. Simmer for 2 hours (in the simmering oven of the Aga) to extract all the flavour.

3. Strain and use this for making the gravy. It is best to do this the day before so that it can go cold and you can then skim off the fat before making the gravy.

4. Once the goose is cooked, remove the goose and grill rack from the roasting pan. Pour off the fat, leaving about 2 tablespoonfuls in the tin.

5. Blend 1 heaped tbs of plain flour into the fat left in the roasting tin on the simmering plate or on the hob on medium heat.

6. Allow to cook for a minute and then gradually add the stock, or wine stirring as it thickens and cooks.

7. Allow to boil for 2-3 minutes to thoroughly cook the flour. Check the seasoning and serve in a warm gravy boat.

Prawn and Apple Starter

This is a simple starter that I adapt to the contents of the refrigerator and the fruit bowl! I think we all stock up with frozen prawns at Christmas, but this is great with fresh prawns too, with or without shells. I'm lazy so I use shelled prawns and just use a few that are still in their shells for garnish!

Ingredients:

40g Butter
3 tbs Oil
400g Prawns
3 Cox's orange pippins
1 Bunch Spring onions
4cm. Root ginger
Zest and juice of an orange
Optional:
50g Lexia raisins
50g Nuts, walnuts or pinenuts
A handful of your favourite herb, chopped (I like basil)

Method:

1. Quarter, core and dice the apples. Trim and chop the spring onions. Peel and grate the root ginger.

2. Heat the oil and butter together in a roasting tin on the floor of the roasting oven or in a heated wok on the hob.

3. Add the onions, apple and ginger. Cook until they just start to take colour.

4. Add the rest of the ingredients. If you are using cooked prawns heat the mixture thoroughly.

5. If you are using fresh prawns cook the mixture for a little longer to cook the prawns through.

6. Check the seasoning and stir in the herbs.

7. Serve in individual ramekin dishes with warm French bread to soak up the juice.

Plum Sauce

Ingredients:

400g Plums
1 Onion
1/2 Stick cinnamon
6 Juniper berries crushed
3 tbs Wine or fruit vinegar
100g Soft brown sugar
4 tbs Gin

Method:

1. Halve and stone the plums. Cut them up and chop the onion. Place these in a saucepan with the cinammon, juniper berries, vinegar and 2-3 tbs of water.

2. Bring to the boil and then simmer until they are tender (in the simmering oven of the Aga).

3. Stir in the sugar and the gin to taste. Remove the cinnamon stick and sieve the sauce.

4. Reheat the sauce and reduce if necessary.

5. This can be made beforehand and kept in the refrigerator. Then just reheat the sauce when necessary (in the simmering oven of the Aga!)

6. Or you might like to serve a Plum Chutney instead:-

Plum Chutney

Ingredients:

250g Plums
250g Apples
2 Onions
1 cup Raisins
1 cup Soft Brown Sugar
1tps Ginger
1tps Allspice
1/4 tps Cayenne Pepper
4 Cloves
1tps Mustard
1/4 tps Grated Nutmeg
Salt
30ml Vinegar

Method:

1. Stone and chop the plums.
   Peel, core and chop the apples.

2. Place all the ingredients together
   in a large saucepan.

3. Bring to the boil and cook until
   the ingredients have pulped
   down to a rich chutney.

4. If it needs to be reduced further,
   place it on the floor of the
   roasting oven, uncovered and
   boil until it is as thick as you
   want. Do keep an eye on it as it
   will catch quite quickly if left for
   too long.

5. Bottle and keep. The chutney
   improves with time!

Aga: Place on the floor of the
roasting ove for 20 minutes to start it
all cooking and then put in the
simmering oven and leave for at
least an hour.

Electric or Gas:
Once the mixture has come to the
boil reduce the heat and cook until
the ingredients have cooked and
reduced to the right consistency.

Cranberry Festive Potatoes

Put 3-4 finely chopped spring onions, a handful of fresh cranberries and a knob of butter in a small ovenproof dish and cook.

Cook in the roasting oven for 10 minutes until the onions are soft, but the cranberries are still firm, or in a sauté pan on the hob.

Stir this into a pan of well mashed creamy potatoes, so that you have a ripple effect.

This looks very festive and it gives a nice bite to the potatoes.

Sprouts go Nuts

Ingredients:

600g Sprouts
50-100g Toasted pinenuts (Or your favourite nut, chopped)
200 ml. Greek yogurt

Method:

1. Boil the sprouts for 3-4 minutes in salted water.

2. While the sprouts are cooking toast the pinenuts in the roasting oven or in a frying pan on the hob. Keep stirring to ensure that they brown evenly. If cooking the nuts in the oven, give them a shake every few minutes.

3. Once the sprouts are cooked, drain them well.

4. Place them in the food processor and whiz to a puree. If you want it super smooth you can sieve it as well!

5. Return to the saucepan and add enough yogurt to give a smooth mixture and fold in the nuts check seasoning and serve.

This can be frozen and reheated on Christmas Day.

Red Cabbage

This is just my favourite vegetable, which is why I include it in demonstrations so often. It is so forgiving if you forget it - it can sit in the simmering oven for hours, just developing more flavour! It compliments all poultry, game, pork or ham so well - it is good for counteracting any fatty meat.

Ingredients;

1/2 medium Red Cabbage
2 Cooking Apples
1 Onion
Rind and Juice of 1 Orange
1tbs Caraway Seeds
2tbs Wine Vinegar
1tsp Sugar
Salt and Pepper
40g Fat or Dripping - Goose Fat

Aga: Place covered in the simmering oven for at least an hour!.

Electric: Cook in the fan oven at 140°c (Gas mark 2) for 1-1 1/2 hours.

Method:

1. Melt the dripping in a large sauté pan or roasting tin.

2. Add the chopped onion and cabbage and sauté gently without browning. Do this on the hob or on the floor of the roasting oven.

3. Peel, core and slice or chop the apples. Add these to the cabbage and onion.

4. Add salt, pepper, sugar, Wine Vinegar, Orange rind and juice and a tablespoon or two of water.

5. Sprinkle over Caraway Seeds.

6. Give the mixture a good stir and leave to bubble for about 5 minutes. Then reduce the heat and simmer gently.

7. This is also wonderful when re-heated and also freezes well.

Christmas Gammon

This is the way my Mother used to cook ham or bacon joints. It gives a wonderfully moist result with a lovely sweet fragrant flavour.

Ingredients:

1 Ham Joint 3¹/₂ - 4kg
1 Onion
1 Carrot
2 Sticks Celery
2 tbs Soft Brown Sugar
8-10 Peppercorns
2 Blades Mace
2 Bay Leaves
Sprigs of Parsley and Thyme

To Glaze:

Demerara Sugar
Dry Mustard
Cloves

Method:

1. Cover the ham with cold water and soak overnight in a preserving pan.

2. Pour off the water, cover with more water and add to this the Onion, Carrot, Celery, Soft Brown Sugar, Peppercorns, Mace, Bay Leaves, Parsley and Thyme. If the joint has a bone pour the Soft Brown Sugar around this.

3. Bring to the boil on top of the Aga or on the hob and then simmer for 30 mins per kilo plus 20 mins.
   Aga: Cook for 15 mins.
   on the floor of the roasting oven and then transfer to the simmering oven for the rest of the cooking time.

4. Remove from the heat and allow the joint to cool in the water.

5. When it is cold remove from the water. Remove the skin from the joint and mix together 2tbs of Demerara to 1tbs Dry Mustard, press the mixture firmly onto the fat of the joint. If you wish you can also decorate the ham by cutting squares into the fat and stud with cloves.

6. Place in the roasting tin with a little of the liquid in the base of the tin and bake for approx 45 mins.-1 hour until the mustard and sugar have glazed the ham and it is thoroughly heated through.

Aga: In the roasting oven or the baking oven for a little longer and it will happily stay in the simmering oven until needed once heated through.

Electric fan oven:170°c (Gas mark 6)

7. Allow to rest for 15-20 mins. before carving or allow to cool completely and serve cold with chutney and salads. The plum sauce goes well with ham too or a Cumberland sauce or a Cranberry sauce.

Turkey Cakes (or Walnut and Stilton Cakes)

This is a great way to use up some of the cold turkey for a simple supper or lunch. It is delicious accompanied by an egg, salsa and a salad!
For Vegetarians who do not have left over turkey, these convert beautifully into Stilton and walnut cakes using up any Stilton and walnuts! Simply omit the turkey and add 80g crumbled Stilton, 100g walnut pieces and 150g cooked and chopped asparagus or green beans to the mixture instead of the turkey!

Ingredients:

500g Potatoes, peeled, boiled and mashed with butter and seasoning
1-2 tbs Whole grain mustard
2-3 tbs Chopped gherkins
2-3 tbs Fresh cranberries
2 tbs Chopped coriander
1 tsp Grated root ginger
1 Small red onion ,chopped
30g Butter
350g Cooked turkey meat, cut up into small pieces
Salt and pepper
Flour
1 Egg
Dry breadcrumbs
Finely grated parmesan

Method:

1. Soften the onion in the butter.

2. Place the mashed potato in a bowl and add the mustard, gherkins, cranberries, coriander, ginger, onion and turkey. Mix well together and season.

3. On a floured board with floured hands take a spoonful of mixture and shape into "cakes". Place in the refrigerator to firm up for at least 30 mins.

4. Break an egg into a shallow dish and break up with a fork.

5. Put the breadcrumbs in a polythene bag and add some parmesan (to every 4 tbs of breadcrumbs add 2 tbs of parmesan).

6. Coat the cakes first in the egg and the toss them in the breadcrumbs to coat. Reshape if necessary and chill again for 30 mins. or until you want to cook them.

7. Cook. The cakes can be fried in shallow fat for about 3 minutes per side, depending on size. You can then cook the eggs in the same pan , once you have removed the turkey cakes.

Aga cook on a baking tray lined with bake-o-glide in the roasting oven on the floor of the oven for 5-10 minutes. Then cook on the top set of runners for a further 10 minutes. (Far healthier using no fat!)

To cook the eggs on the Aga: place a circle of bake-o-glide on the simmering plate and cook the eggs on this, with the lid down (you can do 4 small eggs at a time). They take about 3 minutes!

Serve with Salsa (the recipe follows) and a poached or fried egg on top and a mixed salad or coleslaw.

Cranberry Salsa

This is a flexible recipe - you can add or subtract any of the ingredients according to your likes and dislikes!

Ingredients:

2tbs Chopped fresh cranberries
1tbs Chopped gherkin
1tbs Chopped onion
2tsp Grated root ginger
1 Clove garlic crushed
2tsp. Whole grain mustard
1tbs Wine vinegar
2tbs Olive oil
Dash of Tabasco
1tsp. Soft brown sugar
1-2 tbs Chopped coriander

Method:

1. Place all the ingredients together in a bowl except the coriander and allow to marinate for at least an hour.

2. Mix in the coriander just before serving.

Mustard Mayonnaise

If you are going to have the ham cold, you might like to make a Mustard Mayonnaise to serve with it. This is a really mustardy one!

Ingredients:

1 Egg Or 2 egg yolks (left over from making the Chocolate Almond Log)
3tsps Whole Grain Mustard
1tsp Demerara sugar or honey
1tbs White Wine Vinegar
150ml Sunflower Oil
1tbs Chopped parsley- Optional

Method:

1. Beat the egg together with the mustard, sugar and vinegar.

2. Beating all the time very slowly add the sunflower oil.

3. Season with salt and pepper if necessary. A tablespoonful of chopped parsley can also be added to the mayonnaise.

4. This is delicious served with the cold Ham.

Mincemeat Bread and Butter Pudding

If you have fresh fruit you want to use, eg satsumas, oranges, pears you can include that instead of the nuts. Peel the fruit, slice it and place it sparingly over the layers of bread and butter.

Ingredients:

8-12 Rounds of bread and butter
Mincemeat
300ml Cream
2 Large eggs
4tbs Rum or brandy
50g Flaked or chopped nuts-
optional
30g Demerara sugar

Method:

1. Butter a shallow ovenproof dish.

2. Spread the mincemeat onto the bread and butter. Arrange a single layer of bread in the dish and sprinkle over half the nuts or add the fruit and then put another layer of bread in the dish and sprinkle over the remaining nuts.

3. Beat together the cream, brandy or rum and the eggs and pour it over the bread. The pudding is always better if it is left it to stand for 30 minutes before cooking.

4. Sprinkle over the demerara sugar - this gives a crunch to the top - and cook:

Aga on the grid shelf on the floor of the roasting oven for 15-20 minutes

Electric fan oven 170°c
Gas Mark 6) or 20-25 minutes
Combination oven 200°c and 180 watts for 12 minutes.

Aunty Mary's Christmas Pud

This is the Christmas pudding I have eaten every Christmas of my life. It is actually my mother's (she was also a Mary, so she must have been named after her great Aunt!) Great Aunty Mary's Christmas pudding recipe so it's a real golden oldie. It is a very light pudding and I find it easier to digest than the traditional Christmas pud. It is so easy to make and is actually made on Christmas Day! The measurements are in cups, so as long as you use just the one cup you can make a large or small pud ,depending on the size of cup you use!

Ingredients:

1 Cup Raisins
1 Cup Currants
1 Cup Glace Cherries
1 Cup Flour
1 Cup Sugar
1½ Cups Fresh Breadcrumbs
1½ tps Bicarbonate of Soda
1 Cup Suet
150-200 ml. Milk

Method:

1. Mix together all the ingredients except the milk and bicarbonate of soda, , and then mix together the bicarbonate of soda and the milk and add this to the other ingredients and mix to a soft dropping consistancy and place in a boilable bowl with a lid, or make a lid with greaseproof lined foil.

2. Place in a large saucepan with approximately 10cm of water in the bottom, sitting on a small trivet. Put the lid on the saucepan, bring it to the boil and then simmer for a minimum of 3½ hours.
   Aga: Bring to the boil on the boiling plate and then cook on the floor of the roasting oven for 30 mins and then move to the simmering oven for at least another 3 hours or until you are ready to eat it.

3. When cooked remove the bowl from the saucepan, take off the

lid, invert the pudding onto a
serving dish.
Do take care as the cherries are
extremely hot it is best to let it
rest for 10 mins. before eating ,
but do take care with those
cherries!

Serve with brandy sauce, brandy
butter, custard, cream or even
home-made ice-cream.

Figs With Mascarpone

I love doing these for Christmas as the juice ends up a lovely ruby red and they make a really refreshing end to a meal.

Ingredients:

1/2 Lemon - sliced
10cm Root Ginger-sliced
3-4 tbs Wine vinegar
150ml Water
100g Sugar
400g Fresh Figs
To Serve Mascarpone cheese or
Cràme Fraîche.

Method:

1. Place the Lemon, Ginger, Vinegar, Water and Sugar in a pan and bring to the boil.

2. Add the Figs bring back to the boil and simmer very gently until tender about 30-45 mins

    Aga: place in the simmering oven until tender 30-45 mins.

    If you want to you can remove the lemon slices and ginger from the juice before serving, if you cut a cross in the top of the fig , you can squeeze this open and place the crème fraîche or mascarpone here so that it sinks into the fig.

Chocolate Almond Log

This recipe can be either an exotic cake or a pudding. It's a variation on a Christmas regular with the irresistible combination of rich chocolate and almonds This can be made in the morning or the day before it is needed. It also freezes extremely well. The small almond macaroon biscuits are great to serve with ice cream or with the Figs. They will keep in an airtight tin for a day or two, making this a very versatile recipe.

Ingredients:

The Macaroons:
2 Egg whites
150g Ground almonds
200g Caster sugar
1 tsp. Almond essence

The Log:
100g Almond praline
200g Plain chocolate
400ml Double cream
3tbs Amoretto
Icing sugar
Chocolate leaves or shapes to decorate

Method:

1. Whisk the egg white until stiff and fold in the almonds, sugar and almond essence. Put in a vegetable piping bag with out a pipe and pipe teaspoonfuls onto a bake-o-glide lined baking tray and cook:
   Aga: On the bottom set of runners in the baking oven for 15 mins, or on the grid shelf on the floor of the roasting oven with the cold shelf on the second set of runners for 8 -10 mins.

   Electric fan oven160°c (Gas mark 4) for 20 mins. Remove from the oven and put on a cooling tray to go cold.

2. Melt the chocolate .

3. Whip the cream and fold in the praline, liqueur and chocolate.

4. Sandwich together the almond biscuits into a long log shape and cover with the cream mixture and give it a bark effect with a fork, decorate with chocolate leaves, and a mini robin if you can find one and finish with a final flourish of a dusting of icing sugar- snow!

This can be made in the morning or the day before it is needed. It also freezes extremely well.
Serve with yogurt or crème fraîche.

Mincemeat Stars

This is an easy and pretty alternative to mince pies! Once the mince pie season is here I seem to make hundreds - no sooner have they cooled, than they disappear! I think they are enjoyed so much because they are a seasonal treat, but if you get fed up with making mince pies this is a simple change. At Christmas, ready made puff pastry is a great standby in either the refrigerator or the freezer and is useful for lots of both sweet and savoury dishes.

When making the traditional mince pie I use a basic or sweet short crust pastry. I sometimes use puff pastry for the tops though and instead of putting a whole lid on I cut out festive shapes with my little cutters. An alternative is a swirl of meringue on top a nice touch is to fold ground almonds into the meringue mix.

Ingredients:

1 Packet ready made Puff Pastry (ready rolled saves time and you don't need a rolling pin!)
Mincemeat
Glace cherries
1 Egg
1tbs Milk

Method:

1. Roll out the pastry (if not ready rolled) and cut into 10cm squares. Make 3cm cuts in from each corner.

2. Place a small teaspoonful of mincemeat in the centre of the pastry. Fold in alternate corners onto the mincemeat. Secure by pressing half a cherry on the pastry in the centre. Place on a lined baking sheet.

3. Break up the egg with a fork. Add the milk and brush the egg wash over the pastry to glaze. Bake.

    Aga on the grid shelf on the floor of the roasting oven for 10 minutes until well risen and a rich golden brown.

Electric fan oven at 180°c (Gas mark7) for 10 minutes until well risen and golden brown.

4. Remove to a cooling rack and allow to cool.

Sarah's Truffles

My daughter Sarah, who is now 26 years old, has been making these truffles every Christmas since she was 6! Sarah has always got completely immersed in whatever she does - in this case it was up to her elbows in chocolate, which also went all over the kitchen! This recipe is great for creating your own little gifts for relatives and friends. In this consumer society a hand made gift that time has been spent on is always a pleasure to receive. All these recipes are very simple sweetmeats that youngsters can make, but I make them too as they provide a sweet end to Christmas Dinner!

Note: Please remember that these contain raw egg yolk, and as such are not suitable for the very old , very young or infirm.

Sarah has developed lots of variations over the years, such as:

Orange

Add the zest of an orange and a good splash of cointreau to the chocolate before melting - Sarah liked the smell of the bottle when she was little, so we added some!!

Praline

For a crunchy texture add praline instead of or as well as the ground almonds (keep the total weight of almonds added the same)

You can also coat the truffles in praline, but make sure that you keep them in an airtight tin or eat them that day as the praline can weep.

Coffee

Add 2 tbs strong coffee to the chocolate as it melts.

Rum and Raisin

Soak a tablespoon of raisins in rum for at least a day.

Chop them finely and add to the mixture.

Ingredients:

200g Plain Chocolate
150g Milk Chocolate
 60g Ground Almonds
1-2 tbs Brandy or other liqueur
(Cointreau or Amaretto are
particularly good)
1-2 tbs Double cream
20g Butter
2 Egg Yolks

Coatings:

Ground Almonds, Cocoa Powder,
Praline, Hundreds and Thousands,
Chocolate Vermicelli, etc.
(If possible put in small pots with lids
for coating)
Petit four paper cases.

Method:

1. Melt together the chocolates,
   brandy and butter.

2. Mix together the cream and egg
   yolks, add to the melted mixture
   with the ground almonds, mix.

3. Cover the bowl and allow to cool
   (in the refrigerator if necessary)
   until firm enough to roll without
   becoming too sticky.

4. Take teaspoonfuls of the mixture
   and roll into small balls by hand.
   Toss the balls in the selected
   coating, this is easiest in a mug!

5. Place in petit four cases and box.

6. Keep covered and refrigerated or
   in a very cool pantry until given
   away - if you can bear to!

Hazelnut and Almond Clusters

NOT a recipe for little ones to do.

Ingredients:

80g	Hazelnuts OR Almonds
160g	Caster Sugar

Method:

1. Heat the sugar and hazelnuts together, shaking the pan occasionally, until the sugar becomes golden brown.

2. Remove from the heat and place the saucepan on a wet dishcloth.

3. Working quickly with 2 teaspoons place 2 or 3 hazelnuts with a little caramel onto a bake-o-glide or silicone paper lined tray and allow to set.

4. Store in an airtight tin until required, can be wrapped in cellophane.

Almond Fancies

Ingredients:

Almond Paste
(Homemade or Bought)
Food Colouring
Whole almonds
Glace Cherries
Granulated Sugar
Sieved apricot jam
Paper Cases

Method:

1. Knead the almond paste and add the colouring of your choice. It is a good idea to wear rubber gloves to do this and to do it on an enamel plate or bake-o-glide to avoid stains.

2. **Almond Kisses:** colour the paste pale pink. Roll out to 2 cm thick. Cut out small rounds and press a whole almond on the top. Place in a petit four case.

3. **Cherry Kisses:** use natural almond paste. Roll into small balls. Toss in granulated sugar and press half a glace cherry on top. Place in a case.

4. **Harlequin diamonds:** colour the paste, pink, green and yellow. Roll out to $1/2$ cm thickness. Sandwich the layers together with sieved apricot jam. Cut into 2-3 cm wide strips and then cut diagonally into diamonds and place in cases.

Peppermint Cream

Whilst Sarah made truffles, Tom made Peppermint creams!

Ingredients:

230g Icing Sugar
1 Egg White (Beaten)
Peppermint Oil
Green Food Colouring
Melted Chocolate

Melting Chocolate

Aga: Needless to say, with an Aga all the melting is done with the bowl sitting on the back of the Aga top.

Electric: Melt the chocolate over a bowl of hot water Or in a microwave at 360 watts for 2 - 4 minutes.

Method:

1. Sift the icing sugar into a bowl.

2. Beat the egg white. Add enough icing sugar to make a firm paste. Add a few drops of peppermint oil to taste.

3. Add green colouring to all or half of the paste, knead the colouring in well if you want green peppermint creams.

4. Roll out the mixture onto a board well dusted with icing sugar or between non-stick paper to 1-1¹/2cm thick.

5. Use small cutters to cut out rounds or Festive shapes or cut into squares.

6. Allow to dry on a cooling tray for 24 hours before packing into cases or a box.
You may dip these into melted chocolate to half or completely coat them.

Done!

I hope that you have enjoyed delving into my cookery book and that there are a few splashed pages as it becomes an old friend! It is so satisfying to create dishes from start to finish and to be in control of the ingredients that you use and eat.

If you have enjoyed my recipes you may also like to join me, for a demonstration or for a tailor-made day or weekend course cooking creating and having fun. It also makes a great present for a keen but cautious cook, who wants to master, the mystery and myths of cooking !

For more information see my website: www.janefittonwilliams.co.uk

Index

Jane's foolproof food

314

Ingredients known by different names

A Joint is a piece of meat!
Aubergine - Egg Plant
Caster Sugar - Superfine Sugar
Coriander - Cilantro
Cornflour - Corn Starch
Demerara Sugar - Dark brown sugar or use granulated if it is for a crunchy topping
Digestive biscuits - Graham Crackers
Double Cream - Heavy Cream
Gammon - Ham
Icing Sugar - Confectioners Sugar
Marrow - Large Zucchini
Mixed Spice - Pumpkin Pie Spice
Plain Flour - All purpose Flour
Prawns - Shrimps
Single Cream - Light or Half and Half
Spring Onoins - Scallions
Sultanas - Golden Raisins
Swede - Rutabaga

Cling film - Saren wrap
Kitchen roll - Paper towel

One pound from the sale of this book will be donated to WILLEN HOSPICE in Newport Pagnell in memory of Linda.

Weighty Matters

I have done it for your own good it is very difficult to buy anything in imperial weights now. We are going metric in the book, but just to keep you in touch, some charts down memory lane!

Metric is universal the world over and there is no confusion, if there is only the one to read.

Conversion Charts

Solid Measurements
(Recommended conversions)

METRIC	IMPERIAL
28 g	1 oz
55 g	2 oz
125 g	4 oz
225 g	8 oz
350 g	12 oz
400 g	14 oz
450 g	16 oz (1 lb)
1 kg (1kilo)	2.2 lbs

Length measurements

METRIC	IMPERIAL
2.5 cm	1 in
10 cm	4 ins
15 cm	6 ins
20 cm	8 ins
25 cm	10 ins
30 cm	12 ins (1 foot)

1 tsp.= 5 ml
1 tbs.=20 ml
All spoon measurements are level, unless stated otherwise.
1 cup is approximately 250 ml or 8 fluid oz.
A stick of butter is 125 g approximately (U.S.A.)
An American pint is 16 fluid oz.

Liquid Measurements (Recommended conversions)

METRIC	FLUID OZ.	ENGLISH PINTS
150 ml	5 fluid oz	1/4 pt (a gill)
300 ml	10 fluid oz	1/2 pt
600 ml	20 fluid oz	1 pt
900 ml	30 fluid oz	11/2 pts
1 litre	35 fluid oz	13/4 pts